SECOND
EDITION

WITH RIGOR FOR ALL

SECOND
EDITION

WITH RIGOR FOR ALL

Meeting Common Core Standards for Reading Literature

CAROL JAGO

HEINEMANN
Portsmouth, NH

Heinemann
361 Hanover Street
Portsmouth, NH 03801–3912
www.heinemann.com

Offices and agents throughout the world

The author and publisher wish to thank those who have generously given permission to reprint borrowed material:

Common Core Standards © Copyright 2010. National Governors Association Center for Best Practices and Council of Chief State School Officers. All rights reserved.

Library of Congress Cataloging-in-Publication Data
Jago, Carol
   With rigor for all : meeting common core standards for reading literature / Carol Jago.—2nd ed.
      p. cm.
   Includes bibliographical references and index.
   ISBN-13: 978-0-325-04210-7
   ISBN-10: 0-325-04210-1
   1. Literature—Study and teaching (Secondary). 2. Best books. I. Title.
PN59.J34 2011
820.71'273—dc22   2011012316

Editor: Anita Gildea
Production: Lynne Costa
Cover and interior designs: Shawn Girsberger
Cover photograph: Don Harrison, GoalCoast Publications
Typesetter: Shawn Girsberger
Manufacturing: Steve Bernier

Printed in the United States of America on acid-free paper
15   14   13   12   VP   2   3   4   5

To PMJ

"If you don't live it, it won't come out of your horn."

—CHARLIE "BIRD" PARKER

Contents

ACKNOWLEDGMENTS

This second edition of *With Rigor for All* would not have been possible without the continuing support I have received from Heinemann Publishers, first when they picked up the book from Calendar Islands, who initially published it, and throughout the years as they continued to keep the volume available through fourteen printings. I owe an enormous debt of gratitude to Peter Stillman and James Strickland as they shepherded a fledgling writer through her first book and later to Lisa Luedeke for her help thinking through what the volume needed to be relevant in its second decade. As always, none of this work would have been possible without the unwavering assistance of my husband, Michael Jago, hater of split infinitives and the verb "to get."

Introduction:
Teaching in Troublous Times

The great world has spun many revolutions in the decade since *With Rigor for All* was first published. Forty-four states and the District of Columbia have adopted common English language arts standards. Young adult literature has proliferated, gaining wide readership among students and teachers. Digital communication is a natural and growing part of every teenager's everyday life.

Despite such changes, much remains the same for English teachers. Students still groan when asked to read demanding literature and still look for ways to pass the class without turning the pages. Assigned tasks continue to elicit knee-jerk complaints of boredom. Teenagers always prefer to talk than listen. Lest you harbor the belief that it has ever been otherwise or are new to the profession and think your instruction would have gone more smoothly if only you had worked in the good old days, take a look at what Peter the Hermit wrote in 1274. "The world is passing through troublous times. The young people of today think of nothing but themselves. They have no reverence for parents or old age. They are impatient of all restraint. They talk as if they knew everything, and what passes for wisdom with us is foolishness with them. As for the girls, they are forward, immodest and unladylike in speech, behavior and dress."

For those of us who work in middle and high schools, the times have ever been and always will be troublous. For me, the "trouble" has always been a large part of the pleasure I derive from teaching. It goes with the territory. The challenge is to help the teenagers in our care come to care about living literate lives. Threatening them with the dire consequences of performing poorly on tests doesn't achieve this result. Demonstrating the intellectual pleasures to be had in the company of good books does. That said, I fear that too often in an effort to make the curriculum relevant we lose the rigor. In our effort to provide students with readings that they can relate to, we sometimes end up teaching works that students can read on their own at the expense of teaching texts that they most certainly do need assistance negotiating.

This is not to suggest that we should stop putting contemporary young adult literature into students' hands, but rather to remind ourselves that we should be teaching in what Lev Vygotsky (1962) calls the zone of proximal development. Vygotsky wrote that "the only good kind of instruction is that which marches ahead of development and leads it" (104). If students can read a book on their own, it probably isn't the best choice for classroom study. Teachers also run the danger of ruining books like Stephen Chbosky's *The Perks of Being a Wallflower* with talk of foreshadowing and symbolism. Such stories are best when gobbled up and passed from hand to hand. Classroom texts should pose intellectual challenges for readers and invite them to stretch and grow. Reading demanding books makes students stronger readers and, over time, stronger people. Rigor versus relevance doesn't need to be an either/or proposition. Through careful text selection—distinguishing between independent reading and guided reading—it is possible to achieve both. The stakes are high. Without artful instruction, many students will never acquire the literacy skills they need to meet not only Common Core Standards but the challenges this brave new world is sure to deal them.

Schooling has long been equated with book learning. While book learning never much appealed to the likes of Huck Finn, teachers cling to the fundamental belief that a school day should be spent reading and writing. Education experts now tell us that today's students are radically different from those who populated our classrooms in the past. Weaned on the lightning-quick access and brilliant images of the Internet, these students no longer have patience for books. Addicted to the constant exchange of texting and tweeting, they need a highly interactive, digital learning environment. The evidence to support this view is powerful and persuasive. A 2010 study published by the Kaiser Family Foundation reported that "today, 8– to 18–year-olds devote an average of 7 hours and 38 minutes to using entertainment media across a typical day (more than 53 hours a week). And because they spend so much of that time 'media multitasking,' they actually manage to pack a total of 10 hours and 45 minutes worth of media content into those 7½ hours." In response, publishing companies are busily at work developing instructional materials that look less like a book and more like a video game. Oh, brave new world, indeed!

In a compelling *New Yorker* article the novelist Nicholson Baker (2010) reports on a year spent playing video games with his sixteen-year-old son. He details the astounding number of times players kill and die as well as the gruesome images that fill their screens. "You are a gun that moves." One game Baker describes is set on Mount Olympus and seemingly pays homage to Greek mythology. "*God of War III* has visual astonishments in almost every scene. You walk around on Gaia's gigantic rocky body. You see her giant stony breast. You climb into her chest cavity and see her stony heart beating. You cut her wrist so that she falls away. The game, to a surprising degree, is about hacking away at half-naked women, or naked half-women. Whenever you see female breasts, you have a pretty good idea that the breasted person is going to die horribly, and soon" (59). I can't help asking myself what effect hours and hours of intense engagement with such games is doing to the imaginations and imaginings of young boys. There are better ways to learn Greek mythology.

It seems to me that students today are a lot like Huck. Rough around the edges, they are instinctively philosophical and actively looking for ways to make sense of their world. When we, their teachers, back away from offering them the richness and complexity found in art, literature, music, and history because that panoply is foreign to students' experience or because the texts are challenging, we abrogate our fundamental responsibility to broaden students' horizons. Few young people will ever head off with Huck and "light out for the territory," but many can take this journey as Emily Dickinson describes "without oppress of toll" through books.

Long before I owned a passport, I traveled through the Florence of Michelangelo in Irving Stone's *The Agony and the Ecstasy* and spent a day with Alexander Solzhenitsyn's Ivan Denisovich in the Gulag. I went to the antebellum South in *Gone with the Wind* and *Uncle Tom's Cabin*. Maybe I didn't understand all the interchapters in John Steinbeck's *Grapes of Wrath* as I gobbled up the novel in two days of nonstop reading, but I suffered with the Joads as they fled the Dust Bowl. I'm not talking here about teaching literature but rather about intense personal reading. Again and again the Common Core Standards say that students must read "proficiently and independently." Why should it seem old-fashioned to ask students to put down their Xbox controllers and pick up a book or to pick up their e-reader and spend time with Tom Sawyer? If young people can find time for seven hours of playing video games and social networking, it shouldn't be onerous to carve out an hour for reading—that is, if their English teachers have the will to work to make this happen.

Apart from a rare few, the young people I teach do not pick up literature with much enthusiasm. At first they groan, "Three hundred pages of poetry!" Then they moan, "I can't do it. Not one word of what I read last night made sense." They always hope that if they complain enough, I will abandon the text for something simpler. Instead I assure them that over the next few weeks I will show them how to unlock this text for themselves. I let students know that the satisfaction they will feel at meeting this textual challenge is an intellectual reward that I would not for the world deny them. Does every student experience this reward with every book? Of course not. But many students who never expected to be able to negotiate demanding literature find that with a little help from their teacher and peers, the book isn't as taxing as they first thought. This dawning realization is an important instructional goal. Students are learning not to fear complex syntax or unfamiliar vocabulary. They are beginning to see that long doesn't necessarily mean boring.

Another goal I consciously pursue is love and respect for literature. In her provocative essay "I Know Why the Caged Bird Cannot Read," Francine Prose (1999) argues that:

> Traditionally, the love of reading has been born and nurtured in high school English class—the last time many students will find themselves in a roomful of people who have all read the same text and are, in theory, prepared to discuss it. High school—even more than college—is where literary tastes and allegiances are formed; what we read in adolescence is imprinted on our brains as the dreamy notions of childhood crystallize into hard data. (76)

Who knows but that without determined middle and high school teachers, love and respect for literature will wither and die? It is a fortunate student that stumbles upon the works of Rudyard Kipling, Robert Louis Stevenson, Cormac McCarthy, Zora Neale Hurston, or Mario Vargas Llosa on her parents' bookshelf or chooses to peek between the covers if she does. But for as long as their English teachers continue to make these enduring stories come to life for young readers, the study of literature will remain a vital pursuit.

In *It's a Book,* Lane Smith invites young readers to consider what books have to offer that nothing else does. Books ask readers to look inward, to examine our beliefs in light of new information, to consider the world through different eyes, to take time for reverie and reflection. I fear we are becoming a solipsistic and hyperactive society that knows little about those outside our circle of electronic "friends" and almost nothing about the world outside our computers. As online advertisers become ever more adept at serving up what we most desire, the breadth of our engagement with the wider world diminishes. The Internet promised to open up the world to us. It seems instead to be narrowing the universe down to our buyer profile. As with fast food, our appetites may be sated, but how much nourishment are we taking in?

The revised edition of *With Rigor for All* offers ideas for making English classrooms sites where students can be nourished by literature—intellectually, emotionally, and morally. Despite their seeming aversion to work, students are hungry for such nourishment. For the record, I feel sorry for people who aren't English teachers. Who else gets paid for challenging young people to contemplate tomorrow and tomorrow and tomorrow?

CREATING A CONTEXT FOR THE STUDY OF LITERATURE

Not all books are created equal. Some have the power to transport us to unexplored worlds and invite us—at least for as long as the book lasts—to imagine living in other places, other times. As S. I. Hayakawa explained, "In a very real sense, people who have read good literature have lived more than people who cannot or will not read. . . . It is not true that we have only one life to live; if we can read, we can live as many more lives and as many kinds of lives as we wish" (1991, 78). When students only consume books about teenagers caught up in the very same dilemmas they themselves face, they miss the chance to experience these other lives.

The popularity of J. K. Rowling's Harry Potter series and Suzanne Collins' *Hunger Games* was in large part due to the opportunities these stories afforded readers to imagine attending a boarding school for wizards and fighting to the death for their town. Neither of these experiences is likely in the normal course of events to present itself to my students in Santa Monica, but reading such books offers students a means of experiencing life without endangering their own.

In *Shaped by Stories: The Ethical Power of Narratives*, Marshall Gregory (2009), Harry Ice Professor of English at Butler University, posits six contributions that the study of literature makes to student development. Students develop:

1. **Intellectual curiosity** as the content of great works of literature offers them the ways and means of delving into stories, and, through these stories, of having a vicarious experience of the human condition far greater than any of them could ever acquire on the basis of luck and firsthand encounters.

2. **Cognitive skills** through the study of literature that supports the critical reading of all texts, the precise use of language, and the creation of sound arguments.

3. An **aesthetic sensitivity** that helps them recognize and respond to art.

4. An **intra- and intercultural awareness** by reading texts from both their own and other cultures.

5. An **ethical sensitivity** that includes the ability to regulate conduct according to principles and the ability to deliberate about issues both in their own heads and in dialogue with others.

6. An **existential maturity** that allows them to behave as civilized human beings in a world where others are not always so inclined.

According to Gregory, existential maturity "is more easily defined by what it is not than by what it is. It is not self-centeredness; it is not unkindness; it is not pettiness; it is not petulance; it is not callousness to the suffering of others; it is not back-biting or violent competitiveness; it is not mean-spiritedness; it is not dogmatism or fanaticism; it is not a lack of self-control; it is not the inability ever to be detached or ironic; it is not the refusal to engage in give-and-take learning from others; it is not the assumption that what we personally desire and value is what everyone else desires and values" (57).

Why Read Literature?

How then is literature different from other kinds of writing? And why is reading demanding literature worth the effort? These are reasonable questions to ask. If it is factual information you seek, there are better places to search than within the pages of a novel. Writers of imaginative literature often stretch facts, playing with historical events, historical characters, and even geography in order to offer readers a different kind of truth.

We study *Romeo and Juliet* not to learn about life in Verona but to experience the power and fragility of young love. History books may offer a more detailed description of racism in Alabama during the 1930s, but the fictional courthouse scenes in Harper Lee's *To Kill a Mockingbird* teach readers, through the eyes of Scout, how prejudice can be so deeply rooted within a culture that even Atticus Finch with truth on his side cannot triumph. Literature offers readers a different way of knowing.

Students need books that mirror their own experience; books that reassure them they are not the only ones to have been bullied, not the first to lose a friend. They also need books that are windows, apertures to other worlds and other times, including the hypothetical future. Without the help of a teacher, many students will ever see through those windows but darkly. They need a skilled teacher to help them see how we all have great expectations like Pip, how we are all on a journey to self-discovery like Odysseus.

One myth I'm keen to dispel is that readers go to books solely for self-improvement. Children (and adults) who read do so not to enlarge their vocabularies or to improve their reading comprehension or to build background knowledge. While all of these things may occur, readers read because it feels good. In her memoir *An American Childhood,* Annie Dillard recalls how it felt for her to read as a child.

> Parents have no idea what their children are up to in their bedrooms: They are reading the same paragraphs over and over in a stupor of violent bloodshed. Their legs are limp with horror. They are reading the same paragraphs over and over, dizzy with gratification as the young lovers find each other in the French fort, as the boy avenges his father, as the sound of muskets in the woods signals the end of the siege. They could not move if the house caught fire. They hate the actual world. The actual world is a kind of tedious plane where dwells, and goes to school, the body, the boring body which houses the eyes to read the books and houses the heart the books enflame. The very boring body seems to require an inordinately big, very boring world to keep it up, a world where you have to spend far too much time, have to *do* time like a prisoner, always looking for a chance to slip away, to escape back home to books, or escape back home to any concentration—fanciful, mental, or physical—where you can lose your self at last. Although I was hungry all the time, I could not bear to hold still and eat; it was too dull a thing to do, and had no appeal either to courage or to imagination. (1988, 100)

Readers like Annie Dillard—and I have known many—lose themselves in books the way gamers lose themselves in *World of Warcraft.* The Harry Potter and Stephenie Meyers' Twilight series produced young readers who lusted after the next installment, loved talking about what they were reading, and had no trouble finding time in their busy digital lives to read. The problem isn't about time at all. It's about desire. Students who don't love books—and I have known many—have seldom experienced the kind of thrill Annie Dillard describes. One reason may be that they don't read with sufficient fluency for the work of reading to seem nugatory and the pleasure to be paramount. Another reason they turned back to their game controllers may be that their teachers weren't quick enough to serve up the next book, books like Philip Pullman's *The Golden Compass* or Bram Stoker's *Dracula.* Maybe the door of possibility slammed behind Rowling and Meyers because there are so few librarians left in our schools or because all over America public libraries, those testaments to the American Dream, are cutting staff and curtailing their hours.

In Defense of Depressing Books

You may wonder why the literature we ask students to read for school often seems so depressing. *Romeo and Juliet* ends tragically. Anne Frank dies young. The jury decides against Atticus Finch. It's true that in complex literature, as opposed to formulaic Westerns and romance novels, the good guys don't always win. Yet expressed within many seemingly downbeat narratives are themes of enduring love and the resilience of the human spirit.

Aristotle used the term *catharsis* to describe how the pitiable and fearful incidents that occur in Greek tragedy arouse powerful emotions in an audience. Though the audience suffers with the protagonist through a series of unfortunate events, viewers emerge from the theater satisfied. Despite the unhappy ending, the conflict has been resolved in a way that corresponds with the audience's experience of human nature and with the ironies of fate. In a tragedy the outcome may not be the one we hoped for, but it nevertheless proceeds logically from the protagonist's actions. At the conclusion of the work, we may feel like Samuel Taylor Coleridge's marriage guest after listening to the Ancient Mariner's tragic tale.

> He went like one that hath been stunned,
> And is of sense forlorn:
> A sadder and a wiser man,
> He rose the morrow morn.

Stories, even depressing ones, help young people prepare for the ills they are almost sure to face in their own lives. Sylvia Plath's autobiographical novel *The Bell Jar* is a good example. Many teenagers, particularly high-strung and high-achieving students, at one time or another flirt with the idea of suicide. Plath's tale about a young writer with tremendous potential who suddenly finds herself suffocating from depression triggers conversations about how students face setbacks in their lives and how they deal with disappointment. I don't "teach" the book—an able high school reader can gobble up these 200 pages in a weekend—but I use it for literature circles. Once one group begins talking about Esther Greenwood's perfectionism, failed relationships, and attempts at suicide, almost everyone in the class wants to read the book. Copies of *Ariel* and other books of Sylvia Plath's poetry fly off my bookshelves. Why pretend that being talented and smart automatically brings happiness? It helps to know that others struggle with inner demons and other ills they don't understand. Books demonstrate to students that they are not alone in their sadness.

Students also need to learn that poverty is less a temporary anomaly than a permanent social ill that has been faced by many other people in different times and places. Richard Wright's autobiography, *Black Boy*, helps readers see how poverty complicates relationships, causing people to behave in unexpected ways. When the nine-year-old Richard is mugged coming home from the grocery store, his mother sends him back outside with a stick. She understands that the world is a brutal place, so rather than comforting her traumatized child, she forces him back out into the street to confront the trouble that surrounds him. The lesson she teaches is not merely of violence but also of survival. Ultimately Richard finds his way on and beyond those mean streets through reading and writing. *Black Boy* allows students to experience the debilitating effects of poverty and discrimination vicariously and to begin to understand why the struggle for economic justice and civil rights is everyone's business.

When the study of literature can accomplish so much, it seems foolhardy for schools to shortchange this essential element of a child's education. Yet all over this country curriculum experts are recommending that teachers focus on informational texts. While recognizing the importance of nonfiction in students' reading lives, the most natural place for students to read informational text is in social studies and science. The Common Core Standards include specific literacy standards in history/social studies, science, and technical subjects. They emphasize that teaching reading is not the sole responsibility of the English teacher.

> The Standards insist that instruction in reading, writing, speaking, listening, and language be a shared responsibility within the school. . . . The grades 6–12 standards are divided into two sections, one for ELA and the other for history/social studies, science, and technical subjects. This is division reflects the unique, time-honored place of ELA teachers in developing students' literacy skills while at the same time recognizing that teachers in other areas must have a role in this development as well. (2010, 4)

Influenced no doubt by a business community dissatisfied with employees who need intensive—and, therefore, expensive—training before they can be put to work, schools are increasingly pressured to ensure that graduates have strong reading skills. At first, the argument for investing in education in order to build a strong economy seems persuasive. Who doesn't want a gainfully employed populace paying taxes to pave our roads and put out fires? Who wouldn't prefer to see tax dollars going to build schools rather than prisons? The Alliance for Excellent Education estimates that every high school dropout costs this country mightily. The way Alliance for Excellent Education crunches the numbers, if the 1.2 million students who failed to graduate on time had earned a diploma in 2008, "the U.S. economy would have seen an additional $319 billion in wages over these students' lifetimes." While such numbers are impressive, equating the value of an education with economic growth distorts the purpose of school.

The AEE's position seems reasonable if one's focus is solely on one's own future financial security. Many of the benefits we've come to expect as our right in a modern society depend upon high levels of employment. Social Security won't work otherwise. If we shift the discussion to preparing America's children to lead a worthwhile life, the calculus changes. Is simply working nine-to-five for forty years what you most aspire to for your children? Or do you want them to have an education that invites exploration of tough questions, inspires challenges to the *status quo*, and somehow prepares them for the unpredictable? Most parents want both. The conundrum for teachers is to avoid becoming so caught up in preparing students to make a living—which starts with earning good grades, achieving competitive SAT scores, and winning a place in college—that we lose sight of educating students to make a life.

In *Not for Profit: Why Democracy Needs the Humanities,* philosopher Martha Nussbaum warns that "with the rush to profitability in the global market, values precious for the future of democracy, especially in an era of religious and economic anxiety, are in danger of getting lost" (2010, 6). I share her concern. The movement to reform education to make the United States more globally competitive (our kids are smarter at math than your kids) seems wrong-headed and even counter-productive. Maybe I simply lack competitive spirit, but what I have always wanted for my students is more than coming in first. I want them to learn about and to think about the world. Nussbaum explains that "world history and economic understanding must be humanistic and critical if they are to be at all useful in forming intelligent global citizens, and they must be taught alongside the study of religion and of philosophical theories of justice. Only then will they supply a useful foundation for the public debates that we must have if we are to cooperate in solving major human problems" (94). Alongside history and philosophy, the study of literature offers a powerful means of understanding the problems that have beset and continue to bedevil humanity.

Elite private and suburban schools are unlikely to replace *The Scarlet Letter* with workplace documents in their English curriculum. There is a very real risk that only the sons and daughters of the privileged will continue to read *The Odyssey* and *Beowulf* while urban public school kids are handed instructional manuals and consumer reports. A democracy isn't supposed to work this way. Odysseus' adventures offer students a useful map for internal navigation. If informational texts come to replace literature in our middle and high school curriculum, we will graduate young people who have never seen Circe turn men into swine, who have never sailed past Scylla and Charybdis, and who have no knowledge of the dangers lurking in the Land of the Lotus Eaters.

And what is more starkly real than the story of *Beowulf*? A king is hounded by a seemingly all-powerful enemy and has no idea why this monster has singled out his land for destruction. Every night the evil beast creeps into his hall and slaughters the best and the brightest of his men. To survive, the men must abandon their leader and find safety in hiding. Despair reigns throughout the land until the arrival of—you guessed it—Beowulf. One of the worst mistakes a teacher can make when introducing stories like *Beowulf* to students is to take the cod liver oil approach, "Drink this. It's good for you. You'll hate it now but thank me later." Abandon all hope of instructional success if you pursue this course. First, the concept of suffering now for later pleasure is lost on most teenagers. And second, most kids I know are very good at just saying, "No."

Before I ever put *Beowulf* in students' hands, I tell them about Grendel and his penchant for human flesh. I paint them a picture of the egomaniac Beowulf—a man able to swim in the North Sea for nine days without rest, dressed in full chain mail and carrying a large sword. Surfers in the class become particularly intrigued. Their experience with the ocean tells them that what I've described is physically impossible. Who is this guy? Or, who does this guy Beowulf think he is?

The Uses and Abuses of Reading Aloud

Once students have some sense of the story they will be reading—and one hopes a smattering of interest in the tale—I begin reading the epic aloud. A gifted reader, whether the teacher who knows the text well or a recording of an actor like Ian McKellen reading Robert Fagles' translation of *The Odyssey*, can make the words on the page come alive for students.

The problem with reading aloud, however, is that too often it is used to the exclusion of other methods for getting through a text. Unless the purpose of the lesson is a celebration of language for a kind of "read-in," teachers should not read whole works of literature aloud to students. Reading aloud has become a popular teaching method for many of the wrong reasons: not having enough copies of a book to send home with students; students' poor reading skills; students' refusal to do homework. As a result, students themselves are doing very little reading. Only a few pairs of eyes follow along in the text as the teacher reads aloud. Instead of eyes on the page, students stare out of the window. Yes, the classroom is quiet and the lesson seems productive. A principal passing by the classroom door would possibly think, "My, what a good teacher." But the only one whose reading is improving is the teacher.

Given this caveat, I almost always begin teaching a work of literature by reading aloud a few pages to my students. My voice helps bring sense to the text and, I hope, creates a model for the voice students will hear inside their heads as they read on their own. Many students' ears don't hear what their eyes see on the page. This opening tactic seems particularly appropriate for epic poetry. Since the works were created to be heard, it makes good sense to begin with the spoken word. As I take up my imaginary lyre and begin reading *Beowulf*, I feel as though I am encouraging my students to perform daring intellectual deeds, take up a heroic challenge, slay their personal Grendel, and bring honor to their people. It is a tall order, but most teenagers seem to have more energy than they know what to do with. What they lack is focus. For all of Beowulf's shortcomings, no one could ever say he lacked focus. One has only to hear a few lines of Beowulf's opening speech to become caught up in his character.

Benjamin Bagby has made his life work the celebration of medieval oral performance. His tour de force is a rendering of *Beowulf* in song with accompanying reconstructed Anglo-Saxon harp. The performance has been captured on DVD and is available on the artist's website at www.bagby beowulf.com. Even without understanding the Old English, my students were captivated by Bagby's mesmerizing presence. It gave them a sense of what it might have felt like to hear the work a thousand years ago.

With seventh graders I employ a similar opening technique to introduce stories from Rudyard Kipling's *The Jungle Book*. Students typically bring a superficial awareness of Mowgli from the Disney cartoon character but find Kipling difficult to read on their own. While my oral interpretation of the first page of "Mowgli's Brothers" is no match for the iconic—though hard to find—BBC recording by Ian Richardson, a short period of reading aloud suffices to pique students' interest. To help students transfer the cadence and tone of my voice to the page, I read for ten minutes and then have them read silently for twenty minutes.

At the end of the twenty minutes, I invite students to review what they have read by performing a short reader's theater script of the text.

Readers' Theater Script adapted from "Mowgli's Brothers"

By Rudyard Kipling (adapted by Carol Jago)

Father Wolf: Man! A man's cub. Look!

Narrator: Directly in front of him, holding on by a low branch, stood a naked brown baby who could just walk—as soft and as dimpled a little atom as ever came to a wolf's cave at night. He looked up into Father Wolf's face and laughed.

Mother Wolf: Is that a man's cub? I have never seen one. Bring it here.

Narrator: A Wolf accustomed to moving his own cubs can, if necessary, mouth an egg without breaking it, and though Father Wolf's jaws closed right on the child's back, not a tooth even scratched the skin as he laid it down among the cubs.

Mother Wolf: How little! How naked, and—how bold!

Narrator: The baby was pushing his way between the cubs to get close to the warm hide.

Mother Wolf: Ahai! He is taking his meal with the others. And so this is a man's cub. Now, was there ever a wolf that could boast of a man's cub among her children?

Father Wolf: I have heard now and again of such a thing, but never in our Pack or in my time. He is altogether without hair, and I could kill him with a touch of my foot. But see, he looks up and is not afraid.

Narrator: The moonlight was blocked out of the mouth of the cave, for Shere Khan's great square head and shoulders were thrust into the entrance.

Tabaqui: My lord, my lord, it went in here!

Father Wolf: Shere Khan does us great honor. What does Shere Khan need?

Shere Khan: My quarry. A man's cub went this way. Its parents have run off. Give it to me.

Narrator: Shere Khan had jumped at a woodcutter's campfire, as Father Wolf had said, and was furious from the pain of his burned feet. But Father Wolf knew that the mouth of the cave was too narrow for a tiger to come in. Even where he was, Shere Khan's shoulders and forepaws were cramped for want of room, as a man's would be if he tried to fight in a barrel.

Father Wolf: The Wolves are a free people. They take orders from the Head of the Pack, and not from any striped cattle-killer. The man's cub is ours—to kill if we choose.

Shere Khan: Ye choose and ye do not choose! What talk is this of choosing? By the bull that I killed, am I to stand nosing into your dog's den for my fair dues? It is I, Shere Khan, who speaks!

Narrator: The tiger's roar filled the cave with thunder. Mother Wolf shook herself clear of the cubs and sprang forward, her eyes, like two green moons in the darkness, facing the blazing eyes of Shere Khan.

Mother Wolf: And it is I, Raksha [The Demon], who answers. The man's cub is mine, Lungri—mine to me! He shall not be killed. He shall live to run with the Pack and to hunt with the Pack; and in the end, look you, hunter of little naked cubs—frog-eater—fish-killer—he shall hunt thee! Now get hence, or by the Sambhur that I killed (I eat no starved cattle), back thou goest to thy mother, burned beast of the jungle, lamer than ever thou camest into the world! Go!

As students engage in a dramatic reading, taking on the personas of the characters, their understanding of character motivation always seems to deepen. Class discussion inevitably ensues regarding the Mother Wolf's defense of Mowgli. Why is she so immediately protective? What is there about Mowgli that appeals to her maternal instinct?

Because the tiger, Shere Khan, the brown bear, Baloo, and the black panther, Bagheera, are important characters throughout the Mowgli stories, I have students copy these names onto sticky notes and take no more than thirty seconds to sketch their impressions of the animals. The notes are then pasted inside the book cover for easy reference. I then assign the rest of the story for homework, noting the point (about halfway through) where ten years elapse between paragraphs. It's always a good idea to warn students of markers that, if missed, will seriously impair their comprehension.

Another path to *The Jungle Book* is through Neil Gaiman's Newbery Medal–winning young-adult novel, *The Graveyard Book*. While *The Graveyard Book* is a slim volume with lots of space on the page, extended dialogue, and occasional illustrations, the Penguin edition of *The Jungle Book* contains close to 200 pages of dense prose and curious nineteenth-century poetry. In his afterword, Gaiman acknowledges the debt he owes Rudyard Kipling and the irrepressible Mowgli, who served as a model for *The Graveyard Book's* main character Bod, short for Nobody. Bod was raised not like Mowgli by wolves but by graveyard ghosts. Gaiman's charmingly ghoulish coming-of-age story can help pave the way for reading *The Jungle Book*.

When Kipling fell out of favor with the literary establishment for his colonialist views, the only story from *The Jungle Book* that continued to be widely anthologized was "Rikki-tikki-tavi." While this helpful-animal story about a friendly mongoose is a charming tale, "Rikki-tikki-tavi" is a slight thing compared with "Toomai of the Elephants," "The White Seal," or the Mowgli stories. It breaks my heart that most children only know Mowgli as a cartoon character cavorting with animals. When given the opportunity to read Kipling for themselves, middle school students have plenty to say about beastly behavior and natural folly.

Why Analyze Literature?

Some young readers object to any analysis of literature. "Just let me read!" they wail, wondering why teachers and textbooks feel compelled to interrupt the pleasure of their reading with bothersome questions. Yet probing questions invite them to consider aspects of the text they may have rushed past. The questions point the way to important or puzzling lines, introducing areas of debate and inviting diverse interpretations. I try not to think of analysis as dissection—carving up a text as you would a frog in biology—but instead as careful scrutiny of a living frog. Examine the text from many angles. Consider the music of the language. Measure what you are reading against what you already know. You take pleasure in listening to favorite songs again and again. The same can be true of poems and stories. Each time you return and reread, they open up a bit more, like a flower opening up in the sun. Literary analysis should not be painful for either the poem or the reader. We don't need to do violence to a work of art in order to understand it.

In an article titled "Reconceiving Beowulf: Poetry as Social Praxis," John D. Niles (1998), professor of English at the University of California, Berkeley, explores the implications of epic poetry for contemporary readers:

> Oral poetic performances are often known for their magnificent displays of technical skill. Perhaps more importantly, however, they constitute a praxis affecting the way people think and act. The occasions of oral poetry provide a site where things happen, where power is declared or invoked,

where issues of importance in a society are defined and contested. Oral poetry consists of creative acts whereby a mental order is produced or reaffirmed or one order is substituted for another. (143)

I would like to imagine that my reading of the first two hundred lines of *Beowulf* is a "magnificent display of technical skill," but however flawed it may be, it does seem to "provide a site where things happen." When I asked my students to comment on Professor Niles' assertion in terms of the poetic performance of the singer in King Hrothgar's hall, tenth-grader Lisa Chen wrote, "When the poet sings, he stresses the importance of war and victory in Hrothgar's society. Power is declared and the poet invokes men to fight for glory and fame. He reshapes the bloodshed and killings to fit the mold of an ideal society. The poet is doing something really important here because he builds up everyone's courage to do more daring deeds."

Lisa has gone to the heart of the matter. The first purpose of an epic poem is to entertain, to tell a story. But close at the heels of pleasure is the message that no careful listener can avoid. We, too, must define and contest the "issues of importance" for our own society. We, too, must become heroes. Niles goes on to explain that:

> Works like the Homeric poems or *Beowulf* are not just cultural items to stuff into one's suitcase, "great books" to be checked off a list of things to know. In their manifold reiterations, whether in public performance or private reading, whether they are granted patronage by the great or find a more humble welcome, they involve the collaboration of many individuals. They are the result of a collective even restive engagement with the question of what wisdom is in a world that may seem stable or may seem at risk of spinning out of control. (160)

Inevitably our discussion of a world at risk of "spinning out of control" leads to the comparison of epic poetry with hip-hop lyrics. My students speak eloquently and can quote exhaustively from lyrics they assert are today's epic poetry. They are articulate in their defense of this art form as their generation's contribution to the oral tradition. Tenth-grader James Washington drew the class' attention to the passage in which Grendel is first introduced:

A powerful monster, living down
In the darkness, growled in pain, impatient
As day after day the music rang
Loud in that hall, the harp's rejoicing
Call and the poet's clear songs, sung
Of the ancient beginnings of us all, recalling
The Almighty making the earth, shaping
These beautiful plains marked off by oceans,

Then proudly setting the sun and moon
To glow across the land and light it;
The corners of the earth were made lovely with trees
And leaves, made quick with life, with each
Of the nations who now move on its face. And then
As now warriors sang of their pleasure:
So Hrothgar's men lived happy in his hall
Till the monster stirred, that demon, that fiend,
Grendel, who haunted the moors, the wild
Marshes, and made his home in a hell
Not hell but earth. He was spawned in that slime,
Conceived by a pair of those monsters born
Of Cain, murderous creatures banished
By God, punished forever for the crime of Abel's death.

Then James asked the class to compare these lines with the lyrics of Tupac Shakur. He played for us "Words of Wisdom" from the album *2Pacalypse Now* and asked us to notice the way Tupac describes himself in these lyrics. Tupac's speaker calls himself "America's nightmare," whose purpose it is to remind the oppressors of what they have done to the oppressed. He says that society should be afraid of him because he intends to avenge "four-hundred-plus years of mistreatment." Tupac warns that society should be running from him and should try to silence him.

It was an uncanny moment, disconcerting for a teacher intent upon instilling traditional values and uncomfortable with gangsta rap. Still, there was powerful learning going on here. James recognized the existential unfairness of Grendel's position. What had Grendel done to be cast as the monster? Even before reading John Gardner's novel *Grendel*—something we would be doing in the weeks to come—this student sympathized with the monster and recognized the barbarity within Hrothgar's "civilized" world. Not bad reading for a fifteen-year-old. James' response sent me to the Internet to read more of Tupac Shakur's lyrics. The more I read, the more I was reminded of the lines in *Beowulf* where Grendel "snatched up thirty men, smashed them / Unknowing in their beds and ran out with their bodies, / The blood dripping behind him, back / To his lair, delighted with his night's slaughter." Hrothgar, the king, "wept, fearing / The beginning might not be the end."

We discussed in class the underlying ideas about violence, about exclusion, about love that both the author of *Beowulf* and the hip-hop superstar expressed. This was a heterogeneous group of tenth-grade students, some already college-bound in their minds, others more intent upon getting through high school with as little effort as possible. James, for example, was failing every class he was enrolled in apart from English but was enormously self-confident. Popular and handsome, this African American young man strolled in late to class with a girl on each arm. Tim, on the other hand, was an extremely successful student who for all his intellectual prowess always seemed clueless when it came to getting along with his peers. Tim managed in almost every classroom conversation to offend someone and, as a result, had a difficult time getting others to hear what he had to say. Both Melissa and Lisa were outspoken young women, fearless when it came to standing up for their opinions.

Melissa: Grendel kills because that's what he was born to do. Sure it's gross to read, but he's a monster and monsters kill. Besides, I'll bet one of the reasons people still read *Beowulf* is for the bloody parts.

Tim: Well, I don't think it's fair. In fact, the whole story of Cain and Abel bothers me. Cain killed Abel because God turned His back on Cain's vegetables or something. All Grendel did wrong was to be born one of Cain's descendants. That sucks.

Lisa: Yeh, it sucks but that doesn't make it right for Grendel to kill innocent sleeping men.

James: Not right but I can see why he does it. To me, Grendel's life is a lot like the life Tupac raps about. I mean, when Tupac says that society made him what he is, he's saying that when everybody who sees you hates you, you start to hate back, and when all you know is hate, killing feels normal.

Me: But that doesn't make the killing a virtue, does it? I hate the way rappers glorify violence.

Tim: No, but I'm with James here. If I grew up all hairy and ugly like Grendel and never had anyone to teach me any different maybe I'd start having soldiers for lunch, too.

Melissa: That's sick.

Me: Wait, think about what Tim is saying, Melissa.

Suddenly any need to defend analyzing literature as a worthwhile endeavor, relevant to their contemporary lives, evaporated. Thinking about Marshall Gregory's defense of the study of literature, I saw that in the course of their reading and discussion of *Beowulf* my students had developed intellectual curiosity. Aesthetic and ethical sensitivity are hard to measure. So is ethical maturity. But I believe these tenth graders are well on their way to developing the habits of mind Marshall Gregory describes.

In his essay "The Ethics of Teaching Literature," Wayne Booth (1998) has a section called, "Why English Teachers, If They Teach Stories Ethically, Are More Important to Society Than Even the Best Teachers of Latin or Calculus

The bilingual edition of Seamus Heaney's translation of *Beowulf* invites students to compare on facing pages the Old English version with the modern translation. Heaney captures perfectly the four-beat line and caesura, "Over the waves, with the wind behind her / and foam at her neck, she flew like a bird." I can hardly imagine using any other version to teach the epic any more.

or History." Booth argues that literature is central to the education of every child and asserts that through stories young people can learn to confront ethical dilemmas. "Our most powerful ethical influences—except perhaps for parental modeling—are stories: it is in responding to, taking in, becoming transported by story that character is formed, for good or ill" (48). I would like to think that by shepherding thirty-two years of students through some of the finest literature in the world that I have made some contribution to their characters. I pray it has been for good.

Developing Proficient, Independent Readers

*I*n his 1987 Nobel Prize acceptance speech, Joseph Brodsky explained that:

> In the history of our species, the book is an anthropological development, similar essentially to the invention of the wheel. Having emerged in order to give us some idea not so much of our origins as of what the Sapiens is capable of, a book constitutes a means of transportation through the space of experience, at the speed of turning a page.

The challenge for most teachers as they contemplate assigning demanding literature is to help students operate this curious means of transportation and how to get them turning those pages. Most English teachers agree that moving through "the space of experience" is essential. Our greatest struggle is figuring out how to keep young readers moving. You know the litany: My students won't read anything longer than two hundred pages. The vocabulary in Charles Dickens is too hard for English learners. Description turns sixth-grade boys (or seventh-grade, or eighth-grade, or . . .) off. The print is too small. The setting is outside my students' experience. There is always a good reason for not doing something difficult. We owe it to students to stop making excuses and to start teaching them how to read demanding literature.

I have made a huge number of mistakes over the years. I believe I learned from these wrong turnings and hope to have been quick to adjust—sometimes between periods two and three. One wrong turn I took was to attempt to urge students to read by furnishing them with shorter, easier, funnier books. I worked hard to find novels I thought students would find engaging. Again and again I found that while such stories with contemporary characters and easy-to-read

You don't know about me without you have read a book by the name of The Adventures of Tom Sawyer; but that ain't no matter.

—Mark Twain,
Adventures of
Huckleberry Finn
(1885)

text made for wonderful independent reading choices, they lacked the substance for rich classroom conversations. It reminded me of my experience in adult book clubs. Whenever my book club chose a rollicking good read like a Michael Connelly novel or Ruth Rendell mystery, we talked for a few minutes about how we all loved the book and quickly moved on to talking about our families or school. On the other hand, when we challenged ourselves to read something meatier like Orhan Pamuk's *Snow* or José Saramago's *Blindness,* two hours were barely enough time to scratch the surface of all there was to discuss.

Recreational reading plays an important role in students' development as readers. It strengthens their fluency, builds confidence, and widens their knowledge of the world. Even relatively trashy books like Cecily von Ziegesar's Gossip Girls series exposes readers to New York lives much different from their own. But the kinds of books that stimulate powerful discussion do more than tell a compelling story. They challenge us to re-examine our beliefs, to tread on dangerous ground, to consort with heroes and monsters. While such books are more difficult to read, they are the ones that we never quite forget, that haunt us long past when the last page has been read. Those are the books that work best for classroom study.

How a Teacher's Knowledge Can Interfere

Even excellent teenage readers are daunted by the vocabulary, syntax, and cultural background encompassed in a Shakespeare play or Joseph Conrad novel. It is easy for English teachers to forget this. Often we know a text so well that it is hard to imagine what students might find confusing. Can you remember the first Shakespeare play you tried reading on your own? Do you recall your first time through *The Sound and the Fury* or *Heart of Darkness*? Did you or did you not resort to CliffsNotes or SparkNotes? Have you actually ever finished reading *Bleak House, Tristam Shandy,* or *Vanity Fair*? I am not trying to make you feel guilty but rather to remind you that while you may be an expert reader of the texts you commonly teach, you weren't always one.

Experienced teachers have often read a play or novel that they teach anywhere from five to thirty times. The first time may have been in middle or high school, the second in college, and, once they began teaching, every year thereafter. I am quite sure I have read *Julius Caesar* at least twenty-eight times. Given our own repeated exposure, it's easy to overlook just how difficult the books we place in students' hands often are. And navigating the first forty pages is typically the toughest task.

Most veteran teachers have had an experience similar to the one described by Michael Smith, a former high school English teacher, currently a professor at Rutgers University's Graduate School of Education.

I used to torture my students with *The Scarlet Letter.* That's ironic because I loved the book. Every semester I taught, I reread it, and the book rewarded every rereading. I'd come away with a more complete understanding of how well-crafted it was. And, of course, I wanted to share my insights with my students.

On about the tenth or eleventh reading, I discovered a hat motif (the "steeple-crowned" hats of the Puritan men, the contrast between the "skull-cap" of the Reverend John Wilson and the feather in Governor Bellingham's hat, and so on). Hard to believe I had missed it for so long. So among the lists my students were keeping in their notes was a list of hats.

I worked hard. I was enthusiastic. I wanted to give my students textual power by modeling what could be done in a close reading. I tried to engage them in the discussion of symbols and motifs that made *The Scarlet Letter* so rich for me. They hated it. And they didn't care about hats. (Rabinowitz and Smith 1998, 103)

Thoughtful, caring teacher that he is, Michael Smith realized that his rereadings of *The Scarlet Letter* were actually making it harder for his students to make sense of the text. While he wanted to talk about hats, the students wanted to talk about why Hester Prynne didn't just leave town if they treated her so badly. They wanted to know how on earth she could be attracted to a wimp like Dimmesdale. And how ever could she have married that Chillingworth in the first place? By focusing on the aspects of the novel that only emerge after multiple readings, Smith—without meaning to—made his students feel incompetent. Too often instruction in English has been an occasion for teachers who know and love literature to showcase what they love and show off what they know. Students come away from such classes—and this is when they are done well—in awe of their teachers but with little confidence in their own ability to read and write about literature.

When we take the symbolic hats approach to teaching literature we run the danger of alienating students from the very thing we want to inculcate—that reading literature is a special pleasure we hope they will enjoy all their lives. In the name of rigor we turn conversations about books into spot-the-symbol searches and, in so doing, unintentionally send students scurrying to the Internet for help. Instead, we need to help students develop the habits of mind that will allow them to unpack demanding literature for themselves.

We also need to remember that few of our charges are planning to major in English in college. For most students the literary education they receive at your hands will be their crowning exposure to rich and demanding literature. According to William M. Chase writing in the August 2009 issue of *The American*

Scholar, less than 4 percent of students enrolled in college today are pursuing a degree in English, down from 7.6 percent in the 1970s.

> What are the causes for this decline? There are several, but at the root is the failure of departments of English across the country to champion with passion the books they teach and to make a strong case to undergraduates that the knowledge of those books and the tradition in which they exist is a human good in and of itself. What departments have done instead is dismember the curriculum, drift away from the notion that historical chronology is important, and substitute for the books themselves a scattered array of secondary considerations (identity studies, abstruse theory, sexuality, film and popular culture). In so doing, they have distanced themselves from the young people interested in good books. (2009)

Effective literature teachers have ever been passionate champions of reading and good, hard books. The 20 percent of undergraduates currently majoring in business need to bring to their future workplaces knowledge of books like Upton Sinclair's *The Jungle* in order to make humane decisions about labor and profit. They need to read George Orwell's *1984* to help them consider the extent to which technology provides Big Brother access to our every keystroke. They need to learn from Jay Gatsby about what money can buy as well as what it can't. Dazzling students with our deep knowledge of the symbols and motifs puts them off. Teachers need to demonstrate for students how to work this magic on text for themselves.

Alerting Students to the Range of Difficulties in the Text

One of the great fallacies about student achievement is that successful students love school. The real difference between successful and unsuccessful students has little to do with their proclivity for scholarly pursuits. The difference is in their willingness to do schoolwork. The causes for this difference are dramatically influenced by the extent to which students buy into the idea that school matters. The documentary *Two Million Minutes* (2007) chronicles the lives of six teenagers from China, India, and the United States over the course of the two million minutes between the end of eighth grade and high school graduation. The filmmakers contended that how students spend these minutes will affect their economic prospects for the rest of their lives.

When results from the 2009 PISA exam (Programme for International Student Assessment) were published and Shanghai's teenagers came out on top, Checker Finn called it another Sputnik moment for U.S. education. "Yes, we knew they were exporting Chinese teachers to teach Mandarin in our schools while importing native English speakers to instruct their children in our language. But we could comfort ourselves that their curriculum emphasized discipline and rote learning, not analysis or creativity. Today that comfort has been stripped away. We must face the fact that China is bent on surpassing us, and everyone else, in education." I don't believe that students in China are smarter than American students nor that they like school any more than American students do. Students in Shanghai are highly motivated to do whatever is asked of them because they know how much success in school matters.

Many of my students are irked by the work: paying attention, doing the reading, taking notes, studying for tests, writing papers. I don't blame them. But students who fail to discipline themselves to these tasks learn very little. I wish it were otherwise. I wish that learning to read were as natural as breathing. It isn't. Reading literature, like learning a language or studying chemistry, takes applied effort. Caring educators have often made the mistake of promoting the idea that learning is fun. From this faulty premise follows the assumption that anything that isn't fun need not be completed. If the assignment feels like work, there must be something wrong with the book, or with the teacher, or maybe with the whole school. In fact learning can be enormous fun and with a good teacher often is, but fun must be incorporated into the higher purpose of understanding and appreciating literature.

No teacher with any sense would expect teenagers to love *Crime and Punishment* at first sight. A cursory glance at the 629-page novel sends the fainthearted running for SparkNotes. For this reason, I always warn students that they are going to have to struggle a bit before they will feel comfortable inside Dostoevsky's fictional world. I promise to be there to help and answer questions, but I explain that I can't do the work for them. If they want to know Raskolnikov, it is going to take effort. The intellectual fun comes later when students realize how much this extraordinary character has taught them about themselves. Instead of pretending that obstacles don't exist, I address the potential stumbling blocks directly. Forewarned is forearmed.

I introduce students to *Crime and Punishment* (and similar books) in the following manner:

Length

Yes, *Crime and Punishment* is a very long book. It is also a heavy book. Get over it. Trust me that I would never assign this novel if it weren't a glorious story and if I didn't love it myself. You are going to read things here that you will never forget. Some of the characters you meet on these pages are likely to live with you forever. (Ignore the smart aleck who tells you his house is already overcrowded.) And long doesn't necessarily mean boring. Think *Twilight*.

Vocabulary

You are likely to come across many unfamiliar words in this book. Try not to let that frustrate you. I'll help you learn how to make reasonable guesses about a word's meaning from context. We will also keep a list of the new words that we are learning. Developing your vocabulary is a lifelong pursuit. It will also help you to do well on the SAT and ACT. (Reading a great book for the purpose of boosting one's test scores seems a silly way to behave to me, but if it motivates students to do the work, I'll use it; especially since I know they will get much, much more from the novel than a few new vocabulary words.)

Syntax

Some sentences may at first seem hard to understand. They may be longer than the ones you are used to reading online or in magazines. In some cases or if you read particularly slowly, you may find that by the time you reach the end of the sentence, you have forgotten what was going on at the beginning. I will help you learn to pick up your pace. If the first pages aren't making sense to you, try stopping at the end of every sentence and thinking for a moment about its meaning. See if you can put the sentence into your own words. If not, try to identify where your understanding broke down. Was it hard to tell who was doing the action? Did you get lost in a series of phrases? Mark the spot so you can return to it later.

Unfamiliar Settings

Every novel invites you to enter a fictional world. Finding your way in that world is always easiest when the fictional world has a lot in common with the world you know. The more foreign the world is to your own, the greater will be your difficulty imagining that world. Don't give up. One of the greatest joys of reading is traveling to places you will never see. Who wants to know only the neighborhood where fate dropped you? Don't be put off by descriptions of landscapes that you can't picture. Ask questions. I'm sure others in the class are having the very same difficulty. You may also come across allusions to political figures or historical events you know nothing about. Sometimes these references are essential to the story, but often they are not. Make note of the spot and ask about it in class. If I don't know the answer to the question, I'll help you find it.

Strange Names

I always have trouble at the beginning of a novel when several characters' names begin with the same letter. What I have learned to do is make myself pronounce the names out loud. This seems to separate them in my head. If you are struggling to keep the characters straight, make an annotated list of names on a sticky note and keep this inside the front cover. Some novels include a cast of characters or family tree. Use it. We can create one together as a class if the author hasn't furnished us with one.

Format

While the genre of the novel is somewhat familiar to students, plays can be confusing and off-putting. Start by reading any introductory notes the playwright offers. If you skip this section it will be harder to visualize the actions taking place on stage. Don't gloss over italicized explanations of how a line is to be delivered, either. Often your best clues to the content of a scene are to be found within parentheses. A good example of this can be found on the final page of Act 1 of August Wilson's (1986) Pulitzer Prize–winning play *Fences*.

CORY: Mama!

ROSE: Troy. You're hurting me.

TROY: Don't you tell me about no taking and giving.

(CORY comes up behind TROY and grabs him. TROY, surprised, is thrown off balance just as CORY throws a glancing blow that catches him on the chest and knocks him down. TROY is stunned, as is CORY.)

ROSE: Troy. Troy. No!

(TROY gets to his feet and starts at CORY.)

Troy … no. Please! Troy!

(ROSE pulls on TROY to hold him back. TROY stops himself.)

TROY: (To CORY.) Alright. That's strike two. You stay away from around me, boy. Don't you strike out.

(Exit TROY as the lights go down.)

While this scene may occupy only a very few minutes on the stage when the actors are doing the hard work for you, it may take several readings before you can fully understand what is going on among these characters.

Sometimes a Tortoise, Sometimes a Hare: Adjusting Reading Rates

By describing the minefields, I hope to prevent student readers from getting blown to bits by a demanding text. I also try to prepare them for shifting into a different kind of reading mode for reading literature from the one they use when reading text messages or Twitter feeds. Most adult readers are acutely aware the of the differences between the way they read a story in *Cosmopolitan* (guilty and surreptitiously in the grocery store line) or a trail of Facebook messages (quickly and lightly while avoiding more onerous tasks) compared with the way they read a history book. Many students see no such distinction. Reading is reading. They don't know to slow their pace on the opening pages where every character is unfamiliar; the setting is under construction; the narrative voice is new to their ears; and the plot is yet to be determined. Their eyes move across a line of print and down the page at the same rate with the same level of attention whatever the text in their hands or on the screen.

Three engaging plays for middle school students to read, discuss, and perform:

Day of Tears, Julius Lester

Monster, Walter Dean Myers

The Effect of Gamma Rays on Man-in-the-Moon Marigolds, Paul Zindel

As readers spend increasing amounts of time reading websites, we are developing particular online reading habits. Eye-tracking studies demonstrate that individuals read websites in an F-shaped pattern. Our eyes move first in a horizontal line across the top of the page and then in a second horizontal line, usually shorter than the first. In a third sweep we scan the left side of the page in a vertical movement. Readers rarely pay attention to every word on the page and are likely to move on to another website after the second paragraph (reading less of the second paragraph than the first). Much has been made of this research among webpage designers keen to attract readers to their content and sell their products. As a result, what began as an efficient method for garnering information has become a template for webpage design. The medium has indeed become the message.

English teachers need to help their students understand how different kinds of texts require different kinds of reading. F-shape reading may be an effective way to scan a webpage, but reading the third word on a line less often than the first two is no way to read literature. The matter is further complicated by the fact that students may soon be doing most of their reading on an electronic device. The temptation to skim and scan through every text, whatever its content, will be enormous. Reading Aesop's fable of "The Tortoise and the Hare" can be an amusing way to introduce students to the benefits of slow reading.

The Tortoise and the Hare

By Aesop

The Hare was once boasting of his speed before the other animals. "I have never yet been beaten," said he, "when I put forth my full speed. I challenge any one here to race with me."

The Tortoise said quietly, "I accept your challenge"

"That is a good joke," said the Hare. "I could dance round you all the way."

"Keep your boasting till you've beaten," answered the Tortoise. "Shall we race?"

So a course was fixed and a start was made. The Hare darted almost out of sight at once, but soon stopped and, to show his contempt for the Tortoise, lay down to have a nap. The Tortoise plodded on and plodded on, and when the Hare awoke from his nap, he saw the Tortoise just near the winning-post and could not run up in time to save the race. Then said the Tortoise:

"Plodding wins the race."

Along with providing a vehicle for discussing why slow and steady wins the day for the tortoise as well as for readers, the fable is part of the background knowledge readers are expected to possess. While most children come to class knowing such stories, several of my students were born in other countries. Though knowledgeable about their own cultural heritage, few have heard of Aesop.

Reading on electronic devices is accompanied by the danger of succumbing to what Maryanne Wolf calls the multidimensional, "continuous partial attention" culture of the Internet. In her book *Proust and the Squid: The Story and Science of the Reading Brain* (2007), she describes how the hours spent processing the steady stream of online information is actually reshaping the architecture of our brains. For good or bad, it's happening. The challenge for teachers is to help make students aware of reading habits they are forming. If students only skim and scan, they will never develop the ability to read profoundly and introspectively. Wolf invites us to ponder what is lost and what is gained and to consider the implications for instruction.

In order to help students become more aware of their rate of reading I have them figure out how fast they read. My methods here are quite unscientific and designed only to give students approximate figures. I ask them to bring to class a book that they find easy to read, —not a picture book or magazine but something that interests them and is relatively easy to read. Ideally, it would be a book they have read before. I then have students follow these steps:

1. Record their starting page number.

2. Read for twenty minutes as quickly as they can.

3. Record their ending page number.

4. Determine how many pages they have read.

5. Multiply the number of pages by three to give them the number of pages they would have read in an hour had they the stamina to keep going.

6. Divide by sixty to determine the number of pages they read per minute.

You will be amazed by how many students whip out their graphing calculators to do this arithmetic. I remind students that the difference in the number of words on a page in various books makes a huge difference in the rate of their reading. Here they have a rough estimate of how quickly they move when reading for pleasure. Your strong readers can cover about a page a minute.

Then I ask students to open up their copies of whatever literature we are reading together —*Call of the Wild, To Kill a Mockingbird, Black Boy, Frankenstein*— and to repeat these steps. Invariably, students find that the prose in the book we are reading as a class has slowed them down quite a bit. I let them know that this is a good thing; difficult vocabulary, complex syntax, and a complicated story all contribute to making this text a slower read. I also suggest that in order to enjoy Jack London, Harper Lee, Richard Wright, and Mary Shelley's artful use of language that they might want to slow down even more.

The next step in this process is to have students use their reading rate to calculate how long it will take them to complete tonight's twenty pages of assigned homework reading. For many students this is an epiphany. They never imagined they could actually figure out how much time they need to set aside to read a particular number of pages. You will immediately hear cries of, "Unfair! It's only going to take Brittany twenty minutes and it's going to take me an hour." I answer simply that at least now they know. We talk about the kind of setting that is best for concentrated reading. Some insist they read best with music in the background. I insist that nobody reads well in front of the television. Many report that they leave their reading for English until they have finished the rest of their homework. They take the book into bed with them. I suggest that a semi-somnolent state is not ideal for reading a demanding book and request that one day a week they read first, before their heads begin to nod.

Finally, I have students calculate how long it will take them to read the whole book. Students like knowing exactly how much of their lives they are going to have to invest in a novel. I try to give students greater control over their own success in school. Knowledge is power. If a student knows it is going to take forty-five minutes to read Chapter 17, he can be more strategic about planning his after-school hours. If he knows he has soccer practice until 7 p.m. and fifteen problems to solve due in math, he can see that there won't be much time for playing video games tonight. Or maybe he won't see that at all, but at least I have helped this student determine realistically how long his English homework will take to complete.

Good-Enough Reading

In a fascinating piece of research titled "Good-Enough Reading: Momentum and Accuracy in the Reading of Complex Fiction," Margaret Mackey (1997) illustrates how readers engage in a good-enough reading, striking a personal balance between the need for momentum and the need for accountability to the text. She opens her article with this caveat:

> Reading is an event in time: complex, untidy, and inevitably partial. Often when reading researchers talk about reading they inadvertently or otherwise camouflage the inherent messiness of readers' temporal accommodations to a text by referring to post-reading responses. Such responses apply a retrospective coherence to a swarm of impressions and associations that can only gain any real shapeliness after the reading act itself is concluded. Much reading research and literary theorizing also

magnifies the effect of coherence by dealing with short, highly crafted texts. (428)

As she examined the reading habits of middle school, high school, and university students, Margaret Mackey found that the tolerance for good-enough readings varied among readers. Some favor momentum; others place a greater value on accuracy. But "no reader can entirely ignore the need for momentum; reading must ultimately move forward if it is to occur at all" (429). Instead of calling a halt to their reading while they investigate a detail, good readers create a temporary interpretation that enables them to keep reading.

> [Good readers] develop provisional understandings: they simply take note that something is important and keep on reading without pausing to fret over its complete significance; they provide effective substitutes from their own personal experiences when they cannot immediately make a cultural reference; they carry on even when they are not clear that their understanding of the story is accurate or appropriate, hoping for clarity to develop over time. (455)

I wondered if learning how to do this kind of "good-enough" reading might help some of my struggling readers. I urged my students to proceed with less than complete information, to keep moving forward on the page even if they don't quite understand what is happening in the story. Obviously such a habit can have unfortunate results and leave a reader confused and misled. But the more I thought about how I read, confidently assuming that anything that doesn't make sense now will come clear in the end, the more convinced I became that encouraging students to move ahead with partial understanding would ultimately help them stay engaged with the book.

The story line of a complex novel is seldom a clear path from A to B. The author may choose to begin in the middle, *in medias res,* as in *The Odyssey,* or even toward the very end of the story and take the reader backward in time with flashbacks or other storytelling devices. Sometimes it is the relationships among characters that seem to make no sense and we struggle to understand who is related to whom. Other times, the fictional world is so foreign to the reader—for example, in many science fiction tales where the rules of the universe bear little resemblance to our own—that simply exploring the terrain is a formidable challenge. Experienced readers know to forge ahead, certain that the writer won't lead them astray. Have they missed or misunderstood some important details? Most likely. But the absence of this information doesn't block their forward progress. Good-enough reading keeps students actively revising their understanding of the story as it unfolds.

I hasten to add that there are times when good-enough readings are most certainly not good enough. It would be a disaster to float along through three chapters of a biology textbook, assuming that confusing concepts will all come clear in the end. With informational texts, each piece of data is important to register, classify, and store. New vocabulary needs to be defined on the spot rather than guessed at from context.

There are also times when good-enough reading is not good enough in a literature class either. Mackey explains:

> It is important to note that acknowledging the role of good-enough reading in the real-time experiences of readers is not the same as being satisfied with good-enough readings as the best that can be accomplished in a literature class. Good-enough reading will sometimes suffice for a particular individual on a private occasion, but teachers naturally hope and expect to move beyond that point in the collective readings that occur in the classroom. Nevertheless, it is important to be aware that much of the activity that occurs in the readers' minds, beyond the reach of teacher or other co-readers, is contingent, incomplete, and messy, that this is actually part of how reading works. (457)

"Incomplete and messy" certainly describes what goes on in many of my students' minds as they negotiate a demanding piece of literature. What always surprises me, though, is how often their messy and incomplete readings startle me into new understandings of a book I thought I knew. I'm reminded of a particular group of seventh graders to whom I was teaching Marjorie Kinnan Rawlings' *The Yearling,* one of my very favorite books as a young reader. *The Yearling* was the best-selling novel in the United States in 1938 and went on to win the Pulitzer Prize in 1939. When I discovered old copies of *The Yearling* in the Lincoln Junior High School bookroom, I was delighted . . . and then utterly surprised to see that the tome was 400 pages long. I remembered the book as a quick read, one of those stories that ends too soon. Undaunted, I dusted off the covers and started rereading.

I was immediately aware that my urban students would be bringing very little background knowledge about backwoods Florida, farming, or animal life to their reading of the novel. Most of them could probably identify a picture of a hoe, but I'm not sure they would know what it was used for. Nor did I when I first found the book in the local library, but I had been reading non-stop since I was nine. If I hoped to engage my Santa Monica students in Rawlings' tale, it was going to have to be through good-enough reading.

Instead of trying to fill in the gaps in their background knowledge by telling them about the setting—a practice I have found to be utterly worthless—I encouraged students to construct what meaning they could from the beautiful words on the page. Here are the first two paragraphs to give you some idea of what I mean.

A column of smoke rose thin and straight from the cabin chimney. The smoke was blue where it left the red of the clay. It trailed into the blue of the April sky and was no longer blue but gray. The boy Jody watched it, speculating. The fire on the kitchen hearth was dying down. His mother was hanging up pots and pans after the noon dinner. The day was Friday. She would sweep the floor with a broom of ti-ti and after that, if he were lucky, she would scrub it with the corn shucks scrub. If she scrubbed the floor she would not miss him until he had reached the Glen.

He stood a minute, balancing the hoe on his shoulder. The clearing itself was pleasant if the unweeded rows of young shafts of corn were not before him. The wild bees had found the chinaberry tree by the front gate. They burrowed into the fragile clusters of lavender bloom as greedily as though there were no other flowers in the scrub; as though they had forgotten the yellow jessamine of March; the sweet bay and the magnolias ahead of them in May. It occurred to him that he might follow the swift line of flight of the black and gold bodies, and so find a bee-tree, full of amber honey. The winter's cane syrup was gone and most of the jellies. Finding a bee-tree was nobler work than hoeing, and the corn could wait another day. The afternoon was alive with a soft stirring. It bored into him as the bees bored into the chinaberry blossoms, so that he must be gone across the clearing, through the pines and down the road to the running branch. The bee-tree might be near the water.

I asked students to read these pages and then to write for five minutes about what they could tell about Jody and Jody's world from this opening passage. I told them not to worry about words they might not know but to focus on what they did understand. Writers take great care with the beginnings of a novel, planting the seeds of much of what is to come. (In an odd bit of literary trivia, Rawlings' editor was Maxwell Perkins, famous for his work with Ernest Hemingway and F. Scott Fitzgerald. I can only imagine how many revisions this introduction had been through.) When I saw students' pens stop moving across the page, I read the two paragraphs aloud to the whole class. Then I asked students to turn and talk to a partner about what they had written. They could, but didn't need to, read from their papers. As I circulated through the room, I had to hold my tongue as some pairs—despite the pronouns—referred to Jody as a girl. I took note that this would be an important misunderstanding to put right as soon as possible. I wondered if it had been the sensitive references to the sights and sounds of nature that caused this misreading. Another common error was the interpretation of the phrase "It bored into him" as meaning that Jody was bored. Such misreadings occur often for English learners. And I understand why! Students spot a word they recognize and jump to conclusions. Again I took note to talk later about multiple meanings. It was a delight to observe that most students saw that Jody would rather wander than work. We were on our way. This good-enough reading was good enough for us to go on.

Robertson Davies (1992), author of *The Deptford Trilogy, What's Bred in the Bone,* and many other novels, said in his *Tanner Lectures on Human Values* that

> The great sin is to assume that something that has been read once has been read forever. As a very simple example I mention Thackeray's *Vanity Fair.* People are expected to read it during their university years. It should be read again when you are 36, which is the age of Thackeray when he wrote it. It should be read for a third time when you are 56, 66, 76, in order to see how Thackeray's irony stands up to your own experience of life. Perhaps you will not read every page in these later years, but you really should take another look at a great book, in order to find out how great it is, or how great it has remained, to you. You see, Thackeray was an artist, and artists deserve this kind of careful observation. We must not gobble their work, like chocolates or olives, or anchovies, and think we know it forever. Nobody ever reads the same book twice. (87)

As a reader I have always tended to be a gobbler, devouring books and then checking off a mental list as "read." But as Davies explains, great books invite rereadings. Teachers therefore need not worry when students only seem to be taking in a small portion of what a novel has to offer or when they miss the hat motif in *The Scarlet Letter.* We must trust that if we have done our job well, they will return to these great books later in life and the books themselves will teach them more.

COMPREHENDING COMPLEX LITERATURE

O n December 31 in 1838, Henry David Thoreau wrote in his journal, "As the least drop of wine colors the whole goblet, so the least particle of truth colors our whole life. It is never isolated, or simply added as dollars to our stock. When any real progress is made, we unlearn and learn anew, what we thought we knew before." Every group of students I meet causes me to unlearn and learn anew. I keep hoping that one day I'll get it all figured out, but some new particle of truth always seems to be coloring the water.

A few things have remained constant. During these years I have been mostly in the same classroom facing the same desks, gazing out over the heads of my students through the same dirty windows. On September 15, I hand out copies of *The Odyssey*. Stop by in February, and you will find me reading *Julius Caesar*. Despite these apparently permanent anchors, my course of my teaching continues to evolve. For example, in 2001, when one student, still in something of a state of shock from events on September 11, commented as we read *Beowulf* that Hrothgar's mead hall was like the Twin Towers. I asked him what he meant. Mark went on to explain that Herot represented what Hrothgar's society valued: prosperity, security, and community. The Twin Towers were visible symbols of such permanence for our society. When Grendel attacked Herot he was doing more than simply knocking down the doors; he was threatening everything Hrothgar's rule stood for. The two planes had the same effect on America. Not bad thinking for a fifteen-year-old. I never taught *Beowulf* quite the same way again.

One drop of truth caused me, in Thoreau's words, to "unlearn and learn anew." Another drop was the realization that for many students simply rubbing up against books wasn't going to make them love literature. It began to dawn on me that if I wanted students to achieve the deep literacy I wrote about in Chapter 1 and that Mark was able to draw upon instinctively, I was going to have to experiment with a dangerous practice: direct instruction. Like many teachers, I am by nature an indefatigable optimist, believing in a kind of literary field of dreams. Build the ideal classroom, and they will come. Offer them books, and they will read. While teachers elsewhere have made such classrooms work, I was having trouble ignoring the fact that many of my thirty-six ethnically diverse students were not growing as readers the way I hoped they would. In my own English department I saw teacher after teacher abandon *Great Expectations* and *Huckleberry Finn,* insisting that second-language learners simply didn't have the reading skills to comprehend these difficult texts. Honors students, of course, continued to be assigned both.

This bothered me for several reasons. In September 2010, Lily Wong Fillmore, a scholar and long-time researcher into English language learning, made an impassioned plea at a conference sponsored by the Council of Chief State School Officers to teachers not to dumb down texts for English learners. Worried about the "gradual erosion of the complexity of texts" offered to students, Fillmore suggested that when teachers offer only simplified materials for students beyond the first year or two of their learning English, it is "niceness run amok." She acknowledged that for the first year or two English learners need altered or alternate texts, but asserted that all students deserve the challenge of complex texts. Fillmore's assertion seemed to validate what I had been arguing for years, that instead of searching for substitute texts, what teachers need to do is acquire the reading skills they need to negotiate rich, demanding texts.

The approach Fillmore recommends is supported by research from the Alliance for Excellent Education. In a 2006 report titled, "Double the Work: Challenges and Solutions to Acquiring Language and Academic Literacy for Adolescents," they found that:

> Fifty-seven percent of adolescent English language learners were born in the United States. The large numbers of second- and third-generation Limited English Proficient adolescents who continue to lack proficiency in English in secondary school suggest that many LEP children are not learning the language well even after many years in American schools.

- Of the 43% of English language learners who are foreign-born, those who enter U.S. schools in the later grades are more challenged than their younger peers because of the fewer resources at the secondary level and the shorter time that schools have to ensure that they learn English and master academic content areas.
- Given that these students are simultaneously learning the language and learning the content, they must *work twice as hard* (the italics are mine) in order to meet accountability standards.

We can't be afraid of telling students that they must work hard. In the disturbing book—disturbing, that is, for anyone who believes that education should promote social justice—*Other People's Children,* Lisa Delpit (1995) raises the perennially challenging issue of what happens to minority and underprivileged students when skills are devalued in the classroom.

> A critical thinker who lacks the skills demanded by employers and institutions of higher learning can aspire to financial and a social status only within the disenfranchised underworld. . . . If minority people are to effect the change which will allow them to . . . progress we must insist on skills within the context of critical and creative thinking. (19)

Delpit suggests an alternative to less rigorous, child-centered methods. She goes on to explain:

> I do not advocate a simplistic "basic skills" approach for children outside of the culture of power. It would be (and has been) tragic to operate as if these children were incapable of critical and higher-order thinking and reasoning. Rather, I suggest that schools must provide these children the content that other families from a different cultural orientation provide at home. This does not mean separating children according to family background, but instead, ensuring that each classroom incorporate strategies appropriate for all the children in its confines. (30)

The Common Core and other excellent language arts standards like those of Texas and Virginia are based upon a belief similar to Delpit's that all children are capable of "critical and higher-order thinking." While the descriptions inherent in these standards regarding what students should know and be able to do in order to be adequately prepared for college and the workplace often seem extraordinarily rigorous, the goal of the National Governors Association initiative is to ensure that every child in America receives a first-rate education.

How Stories Work

Lisa Delpit opened a new train of thought for me. Maybe the reason non-honors students did not have the "reading skills" teachers deemed necessary for negotiating demanding literature was that we hadn't taught them very well. I am not speaking here about teaching students how to read but rather about teaching students how stories work. In our urgency to abandon the lecture format, literature teachers may have adopted too passive a role. Clearly we want to continue to make genuine student response the keystone of the classroom, but withholding information about how a story works may make it impossible for some students to have any response at all.

One has only to consider Toni Morrison's *Jazz* or David Mitchell's *Cloud Atlas* to see that truly "novel" texts continue to be written. But authors build stories with a common set of blocks, drawing from a stock of possibilities familiar to any experienced reader: A hero engages the reader's sympathy. A problem develops. A foil appears to allow the reader to see the hero more clearly. The problem intensifies. Help appears. More complications arise, but the hero prevails. All is resolved. Sometimes, in the words of the Prince at the conclusion of *Romeo and Juliet,* "All are punish'd."

While such story structures may be so familiar to an English teacher that they hardly bear commenting upon, this is not the case for many young readers. Some of my students have touched only books that teachers put in their hands and have never been impelled or compelled to read a single one from cover to cover. One approach to solving this problem is to create a vibrant independent reading program within every English classroom. Another is to use compelling literature to teach students how stories work. I do not believe it is a matter of either/or. Students deserve both.

Let me use Mary Shelley's *Frankenstein, or the Modern Prometheus* as an example. Now, I am quick to admit the weaknesses of the lecture format when employed day after day with teenagers. But the first pages of Mary Shelley's novel pose readers with a real problem. The story opens with a group of letters written by Robert Walton, an explorer adrift in the Arctic Sea, to his sister in London. Without a few words from me about the epistolary format and about the way the character of Robert Walton will become, like us, the listener to Victor Frankenstein's strange tale, many students are lost before they have even begun. The simplest of clues and guiding questions seem to help.

1. What do you notice about the dates of these letters?

2. Why do you think Robert Walton writes to his sister if there is no way for him to mail his letters?

3. What does Robert Walton reveal about himself in these letters?

4. Where does Mary Shelley (through Robert Walton) explain to you how the format of her story will now shift?

5. Can you think of other stories or movies that are structured like this?

My questions aim to tease out from students an understanding of how Mary Shelley's story is structured. I think it unrealistic to assume that the average student can simply be assigned these pages to read and that they will figure out the structure for themselves. Victor Frankenstein doesn't start telling the story students thought they were going to hear until page 30. If I don't offer some guidance—a kind of reader's map—through the first 29, too many will give up.

It also doesn't seem fair to teach novels like *Frankenstein* only to students who, through experience as readers, understand how a series of one-sided letters like

Robert Walton's works. When my colleagues in the English department demand that we simplify the curriculum for struggling students and replace classical literature with shorter, more accessible novels, I know they are motivated by kindness. Would it not be kinder to provide all students with the tools to handle challenging texts? Teachers aren't hired simply to assist students who hardly need them. They are paid to find ways that all students can develop as readers and experience the richness contained within the covers of great books.

I tell my students about how stories work. I remind them to pay close attention to who is narrating the story and to whom he or she is speaking. Where appropriate, I point out foreshadowing. I don't monopolize the classroom conversations, nor do I hold back when I feel that students are lost. One tool for helping students understand how stories work is Freytag's pyramid.

The nineteenth-century German scholar, Gustav Freytag, analyzed the structure of ancient Greek and Shakespearean drama, dividing it into five distinct parts. Contemporary plays do not always conform to Freytag's pattern in that the climax often occurs much closer to the resolution than the diagram would suggest, but the model is a valuable tool for analyzing the structure of stories.

Exposition: An opening scene wherein the audience is provided with background information necessary to understand and interpret the action that follows.

Rising Action: An event occurs introducing the main conflict of the play and complications arise that increase the tension and conflict between characters.

Climax: Traditionally situated in the third act of a five-act play, this is the moment of greatest intensity after which the direction of events is determined. It is sometimes referred to as the turning point or crisis.

Falling Action: Events follow as a result of the climactic moment. In tragedy the protagonist's fortune has changed irrevocably for the worse.

Resolution (dénouement in comedy or catastrophe in tragedy): Previous tension is released as the story is brought to its conclusion, and the audience is offered closure on the events witnessed. In comedy the dénouement is the successful unraveling of plot complications. In tragedy the play's conclusion results in catastrophe for the protagonist.

I find it helpful to introduce the idea of story structure by asking students to recall a story they know well. This might be the young adult novel they are reading outside class or a novel I know that students have all read the previous year, for example, Louis Sachar's *Holes.* Sometimes I use a film that most students have seen or a short story that we have all read recently. Together we chart the main events of the story on Freytag's pyramid, taking time to argue as needed

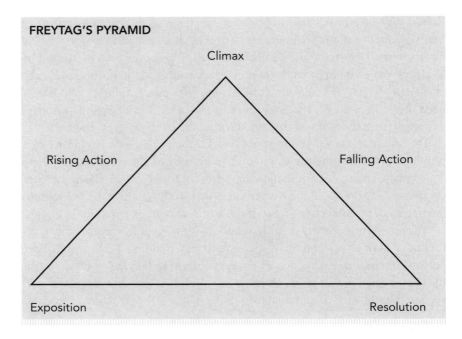

FREYTAG'S PYRAMID

Climax

Rising Action

Falling Action

Exposition

Resolution

about the climax. There always seem to be many different points of view about what moment should be considered the turning point. I am much less interested in correct answers—which are, after all, only my interpretation of the story's structure—than I am in the discussion.

Another approach I have used to teach middle school students about how stories work is to start with a reading of Henry Wadsworth Longfellow's narrative poem "Paul Revere's Ride." The first stanza establishes the context for story the speaker will tell and the second the signal the historical Paul Revere set up to let him know whether the British would row across the Charles River or march out Boston Neck, "one if by land, two if by sea" (exposition). Then the complications commence as Revere must row quietly across the Charles and creep past the British man-of-war in the harbor (rising action) up to the climatic moment when he sees the signal: "A second lamp in the belfry burns!" His ride through Lexington and on to Concord make up the falling action culminating in Longfellow's conclusion that "Through all our history, to the last, / In the hour of darkness and peril and need, / The people will waken and listen to hear" (resolution).

PAUL REVERE'S RIDE
Listen, my children, and you shall hear
Of the midnight ride of Paul Revere,
On the eighteenth of April, in Seventy-Five;
Hardly a man is now alive
Who remembers that famous day and year.

He said to his friend, "If the British march
By land or sea from the town to-night,
Hang a lantern aloft in the belfry arch
Of the North Church tower, as a signal light, —
One, if by land, and two, if by sea;
And I on the opposite shore will be,
Ready to ride and spread the alarm
Through every Middlesex village and farm,
For the country-folk to be up and to arm."

Then he said "Good-night!" and with muffled oar
Silently rowed to the Charlestown shore,
Just as the moon rose over the bay,
Where swinging wide at her moorings lay
The Somerset, British man-of-war;
A phantom ship, with each mast and spar
Across the moon like a prison-bar,
And a huge black hulk, that was magnified
By its own reflection in the tide.

Meanwhile, his friend, through alley and street
Wanders and watches with eager ears,
Till in the silence around him he hears
The muster of men at the barrack door,
The sound of arms, and the tramp of feet,
And the measured tread of the grenadiers,
Marching down to their boats on the shore.

Then he climbed the tower of the Old North Church,
By the wooden stairs, with stealthy tread,
To the belfry-chamber overhead,
And startled the pigeons from their perch
On the somber rafters, that round him made
Masses and moving shapes of shade,—
By the trembling ladder, steep and tall,
To the highest window in the wall,
Where he paused to listen and look down
A moment on the roofs of the town,
And the moonlight flowing over all.

Beneath, in the churchyard, lay the dead,
In their night-encampment on the hill,
Wrapped in silence so deep and still
That he could hear, like a sentinel's tread,

The watchful night-wind, as it went
Creeping along from tent to tent,
And seeming to whisper, "All is well!"
A moment only he feels the spell
Of the place and the hour, the secret dread
Of the lonely belfry and the dead;
For suddenly all his thoughts are bent
On a shadowy something far away,
Where the river widens to meet the bay, —
A line of black, that bends and floats
On the rising tide, like a bridge of boats.

Meanwhile, impatient to mount and ride,
Booted and spurred, with a heavy stride
On the opposite shore walked Paul Revere.
Now he patted his horse's side,
Now gazed on the landscape far and near,
Then, impetuous, stamped the earth,
And turned and tightened his saddle-girth;
But mostly he watched with eager search
The belfry-tower of the Old North Church,
As it rose above the graves on the hill,
Lonely and spectral and somber and still.
And lo! as he looks, on the belfry's height
A glimmer, and then a gleam of light!
He springs to the saddle, the bridle he turns,
But lingers and gazes, till full on his sight
A second lamp in the belfry burns!

A hurry of hoofs in a village street,
A shape in the moonlight, a bulk in the dark,
And beneath, from the pebbles, in passing, a spark
Struck out by a steed flying fearless and fleet:
That was all! And yet, through the gloom and the light,
The fate of a nation was riding that night;
And the spark struck out by that steed, in his flight,
Kindled the land into flame with its heat.

He has left the village and mounted the steep,
And beneath him, tranquil and broad and deep,
Is the Mystic, meeting the ocean tides;
And under the alders that skirt its edge,
Now soft on the sand, now loud on the ledge,
Is heard the tramp of his steed as he rides.

It was twelve by the village clock,
When he crossed the bridge into Medford town.
He heard the crowing of the cock,
And the barking of the farmer's dog,
And felt the damp of the river fog,
That rises after the sun goes down.

It was one by the village clock,
When he galloped into Lexington.
He saw the gilded weathercock
Swim in the moonlight as he passed,
And the meeting-house windows, blank and bare,
Gaze at him with a spectral glare,
As if they already stood aghast
At the bloody work they would look upon.

It was two by the village clock,
When he came to the bridge in Concord town.
He heard the bleating of the flock,
And the twitter of birds among the trees,
And felt the breath of the morning breeze
Blowing over the meadows brown.
And one was safe and asleep in his bed
Who at the bridge would be first to fall,
Who that day would be lying dead,
Pierced by a British musket-ball.

You know the rest. In the books you have read,
How the British regulars fired and fled,—
How the farmers gave them ball for ball,
From behind each fence and farm-yard wall,
Chasing the red-coats down the lane,
Then crossing the fields to emerge again
Under the trees at the turn of the road,
And only pausing to fire and load.

So through the night rode Paul Revere;
And so through the night went his cry of alarm
To every Middlesex village and farm,—
A cry of defiance and not of fear,
A voice in the darkness, a knock at the door,
And a word that shall echo forevermore!
For, borne on the night-wind of the Past,
Through all our history, to the last,

In the hour of darkness and peril and need,
The people will waken and listen to hear
The hurrying hoof-beat of that steed,
And the midnight-message of Paul Revere.

—*Henry Wadsworth Longfellow, 2000*

There is obviously much more to talk about in Longfellow's poem than the simple narrative structure. But understanding the structure of the story Longfellow recounts in rhyme helps build student confidence with the text. I particularly love the image of the British ship's masts as prison bars across the moon. We talk about how the simile illuminates the poem's theme. The website for Paul Revere's House is a rich source of information about the poem and about the historical Paul Revere.

I have had considerable success offering eighth graders extra credit—you know how students will do anything for extra credit, even those who seldom complete the assigned work—for memorizing as much of the poem as they could manage. I offered so many points for so many lines. Most students took up the offer, and we spent a delightful day hearing the poem again and again as they recited portions of the poem by heart. In a 2010 article for *Educational Leadership* called "The Case for Slow Reading," Thomas Newkirk recommends memorization. He believes, as I do, that memorization entails a special kind of knowing, a kind I hope will last my students their whole lives long.

Connecting Literature to Life

I can always tell when students' reading of a piece of literature is losing momentum by the snippets of conversation floating up to my desk. My tenth-grade students had read about half of *Frankenstein,* but they were restless. "Nothing happens." "I fell asleep and missed the part where the monster came to life." "Victor Frankenstein just rambles." And most ominous of all, "Boring." I love Mary Shelley's novel and thought I had been doing a pretty good job teaching the Gothic tale of pride and prejudice (my own interpretation, which I love talking about to anyone who will listen), but something was missing. The students weren't hooked. I knew they were keeping up with the reading because our discussion the day before about Victor Frankenstein's passion for his research had gone well. Their eyes were dutifully passing over the pages, but their hearts just weren't in it.

The lesson I had planned was going to be a close look at Mary Shelley's use of language, examining how syntax and diction created the story's tone. But experience told me that I had better think fast if I didn't want to spend the hour asking questions nobody except me cared much about. Rummaging through my *Frankenstein* files, I found a magazine article about cloning that raised the question, "Are there some scientific experiments that should never have been conducted?" Handing out copies of this essay to the class, I asked students what they thought. Are there some scientific advances that the human race is not and never will be able to handle?

Hands flew into the air. Students saw at once the connection between the moral dilemma of cloning and Victor Frankenstein's creation. They argued that even the obvious medical advantage of being able to clone new hearts or livers would soon be outweighed by the cloning of super-soldiers. The science fiction buffs in the room had a field day telling tales of genetically engineered races destroying the world. I told them about Kazuo Ishiguro's novel *Never Let Me Go* in which the main characters were clones created so their organs could be harvested for transplants. Many students had recently read *Brave New World* and used Aldous Huxley's gruesome society as an example of what can happen when scientists rather than humanists are at the helm.

My role as teacher shifted from Grand Inquisitor to air traffic controller. "First Stephen, then Melissa, then Robert. We'll get to you, Bryan. Hold onto that thought." The hardest part was making sure students listened to one another rather than simply waiting their turn to speak. I complimented those who began their comments with a reference to something someone else had said. This helped. When the conversation turned to the question of whether science might someday make religion obsolete, I thought the windows might explode from the passionate intensity of their arguments. They had so much to say.

At the bell, the room erupted into a dozen conversations. A handful of students grabbed copies of *Brave New World* on their way out. I promised to bring my copy of *Never Let Me Go* to school on Monday. I shouted over the din that they needed to read Chapters 12 through 14 of *Frankenstein* over the weekend. Spent, I collapsed at my desk, reasonably certain that the principal themes in Mary Shelley's novel had finally come alive for these readers. The rest of *Frankenstein* should make better sense now. And to think that some people consider teaching literature genteel, scholarly work. I resolved that at our next class meeting we would take another look at our rules for classroom discussion:

- Students must talk to one another, not just to me or to the air.

- Students must look at the speaker while he or she is talking.

- Students must listen to one another. To ensure that this happens, they must either address the previous speaker or provide a reason for changing the subject.

- Students must all be prepared to participate. If I call on someone and he or she has nothing to say, the appropriate response is, "I'm not sure what I think right now, but please come back to me later."

- No side conversations, copying of math homework, or texting.

Yvonne Hutchison, master teacher at one of the most challenging middle schools in the Los Angeles Unified School District, helped me create this set of guidelines for classroom discussion. She believes that we must assume that all students have important things to say but that many of them are unfamiliar with the rules of academic discourse. A few students seem to know these rules instinctively, most often sons or daughters of teachers. But if we want all students to participate in civil classroom conversations, we need to teach them how. We experiment with the wonderfully vague verb *suggest* when talking about literature. I encourage students to take risks with interpretation by starting sentences with "I wonder if the author is implying . . . " We practice arguing civilly what has been said with, "I can understand how you see it that way, but I . . ."

- Where did you see that in the text?

- If I were in this character's place . . .

- Those lines make me feel as though . . .

- When I compare this with what came before . . .

- I can understand how you see it that way, but I . . .

- Does this word have other connotations?

- I was struck by the line where . . .

- I'm unsure. Can you please come back to me?

Rules of discourse are particularly important during Socratic seminars. Simply putting the desks in a circle won't necessary result in the kind of student-run, text-based discussion that seminars are meant to foster. I find I must:

1. Tell students that everyone is expected to participate at least once during the seminar.

2. Explain to students that no one needs to raise a hand to be called on, but that they should be sensitive to each other, noticing when someone seems to have something to say but may be too shy to jump into the conversation. I give them the words they might use: "Luke, you look as though you disagree. What were you thinking?" If a student with a soft voice can't be heard, I urge other students to ask him or her to speak up. This shows they really want to know what this person has to say.

3. Teach students how to deal with the compulsive talkers in their midst. Pointing out how even motor-mouthed Michelle must at some point inhale, I tell them this is the moment when others can politely interrupt. (I say this lovingly, and the Michelles in the class always laugh. They know that others stop listening when they rattle on for too long.)

4. Tell students that silence is a part of the seminar, too. It means people are pausing to think. If the silence goes on for too long, they might want to turn to the text that is the basis for the seminar and see if there is a passage they would like to ask one another about. They might decide to read the passage aloud.

5. Let students know that I will be sitting outside their circle and that I will remain silent until the last five minutes of class. I will be taking notes about things I observe occurring during the seminar and will share these with them at that time. My comments will not be about the text but rather about how students conducted themselves during the seminar. I focus on the positive behaviors, the subtle way students help one another join in the discussion, naming individuals who did this well.

In my experience seminars work best with twenty or fewer students. With my larger classes I have tried dividing the students into two groups, but it never seems to work quite as well. My presence—my silent, note-taking self, sitting outside the circle—seems to be a key piece of what makes students take the seminar seriously. I have yet to figure out how to clone myself so I can watch two groups at once.

One fall after students had finished reading both *Beowulf* and John Gardner's *Grendel* (the Beowulf story told from the point of view of the monster), I told students that instead of taking a test or writing a comparison/contrast essay about the two books, we would hold a seminar. Since the seminar would take the place of a formal assessment, everyone had to speak up and participate. Students readily agreed. As I wasn't going to be asking the questions or calling upon them, it was up to the students themselves to generate the discussion and, in so doing, to demonstrate to me their understanding of the two books.

Melissa began. "The last line in *Grendel* made me think again about how I felt about the monster. I mean the whole book sets you up to sympathize with him, but look how he finishes, 'Poor Grendel's had an accident. *So may you all.*' That's really mean and malicious."

"I agree. It's blood-lust," remarked Bryan. "This is an evil monster who deserved to be killed."

Lisa saw it differently. "Wait, look at how we was treated in his life. No mother he could talk to. Beowulf out to get him, no friends, no one to teach him how to behave."

Roberto interrupted, "Grendel was just something in the Beowulf's way, something for the hero to slay so he could win fame and have people sing about him."

"That's how it was in *Beowulf*," Lisa insisted. "But in *Grendel* you could see how the monster felt. You knew what he was thinking. In a way I think Grendel was trapped in a role. I feel sorry for him."

The conversation continued in this vein for the next forty minutes. To anyone who delights in watching teenagers learn, the interval was breathtaking. Students listened to one another, probed each other's observations, and made repeated reference to the texts. When it was over I beamed with pride, well disposed to each and every one of them. I let them know that this was the apex of literature study. The exercises we completed along the way were simply preparation for this kind of exchange, for just this kind of conversation among readers about books. After class Melissa came up to let me know that they really should have had more time for the discussion. I often wonder if students are as blunt with other teachers. No one ever hesitates to tell me what I should do better. Of course she was right.

I remember another group of students who had finished reading *Frankenstein*. It was the year when trials were all the rage in Los Angeles: the Menendez brothers, Heidi Fleiss, O. J. Simpson. From all the television time these trials were receiving, my students were experts on courtroom drama and procedures. Sophomore David MacDonald had the idea that we should put Victor Frankenstein on trial for the murders his monster committed. The class loved the idea. Within a few days roles were assigned, teams of attorneys had been to the library for research, robes were found for the judge, and court was in session. Students had the protocols down pat.

My favorite moment occurred when the defense put Dr. Alfred Nobel on the stand. Amy Krasnov asked the eminent scientist if he felt he should be held responsible for the destructive uses dynamite has been put to in the world. Dr. Nobel testified, "Of course not." To which Amy responded, "If Dr. Nobel is not culpable for the destruction his creation, dynamite, has wrought, then how can you, the jury, convict my client, Dr. Frankenstein, for what his creation has done? I rest my case."

Developing Students' Vocabulary

Not all of my students have words like *culpable* and *wrought* on the tip of their tongues. In fact, Amy had prepared her closing statement for the trial of Victor Frankenstein carefully and read from what she had written. She is also a compulsive reader. Students like Amy have large vocabularies, not from studying lists of words but from reading. Don't you often find that it is the readers in your class who garner the highest scores on college entrance exams like the SAT and the ACT? Prior to 2006 the SAT included analogy questions in an attempt to measure students' critical thinking. In my opinion this item type in fact measured vocabulary. (A cottage industry was developed that had its base in tutoring students how to guess on such items accurately.) Readers like Amy have little difficulty with analogy questions like the one shown in the example, but many other students have trouble demonstrating their understanding of the relationship expressed in the stem because they don't know what *tenet, predecessor,* or *recluse* meant. I celebrated when the College Board eliminated analogies from the SAT in the hope that students would spend less time practicing with the item type and more time reading. Rather than focusing on assigning and assessing lists of words, teachers would do better to help students develop the habits of mind that make learning vocabulary as natural as breathing.

Technology can work to our advantage here. No longer do students have to leaf through the pages of a heavy dictionary. They can type *mizzen* into Google images and in seconds an illustration of the sail appears on their screen. When reading in electronic formats, search engines make finding definitions as easy as highlighting the word—if students take the time or if they are prepared to bother. Too often students simply skip over unfamiliar vocabulary. Researchers have discovered that even when we skip a word—which, if we are honest, is what most of us do when we come to a word we don't know—our brains record the encounter. While a single sighting of a word is rarely enough to make an imprint strong enough to allow a reader to know the definition, McKeown, Beck, Omanson, and Pope (1985) found that twelve encounters did.

Avid readers like Amy have repeated encounters with new vocabulary because their reading diet includes everything from Edgar Allan Poe to Colum McCann's *Let the Great World Spin.* As a result, their understanding of unfamiliar words grows with every encounter. For example, the first time a reader sees the word *lorgnette*, one might take away from the context only the sense that the object has something to do with seeing. The second time, there might be a reference to a character holding the glasses and a sense that this is an old-fashioned object given the setting of the story. The third encounter might include some reference to the opera, adding the use of the object to its description. Steven Stahl explained this process in an article called "How Words Are Learned Incrementally over Multiple Exposures":

> As a person encounters the word again and again, word meaning grows at a relatively constant rate, dependent on the features of the context. That is, people show as much absolute gain in word knowledge from an unknown word as they show from a word of which they have some partial knowledge, all other things being equal. We found that students made the same amount of growth in word knowledge from a single reading, whether they began by knowing something about a word or not. Thus, vocabulary knowledge seems to grow gradually, moving from the first meaningful exposure to a word to a full and flexible knowledge. (2003, 19)

Children who are readers add between 3,000 and 5,000 new words to their vocabulary every year through incidental exposure. Consider how much greater this rate of word learning is than the 300 to 400 words per year that can be taught through direct instruction (Nagy, Anderson, and Herman 1987). This is not to say that we shouldn't teach word study, but rather that students who don't read

SAMPLE ANALOGY QUESTION

TENET is to THEOLOGIAN as

(A) predecessor is to heir

(B) hypothesis is to biologist

(C) recluse is to rivalry

(D) arrogance is to persecution

(E) tenor is to choir

much will always lag behind their reading peers in vocabulary development. Betty Hart and Todd R. Risley (2003) report that high-performing twelfth graders know about four times as many words as low-performing students.

Many of the words that students encounter in academic settings rarely appear in conversational speech. When was the last time you used *deleterious* or *vicissitude* in conversation? I'm not sure I ever have. I'm also quite sure that no one ever taught me these words through a list of words. I have simply met them again and again when reading in various contexts.

To help my students build their vocabulary, I ask them to keep a running list as they read unfamiliar words. An easy way to facilitate this process is to hand out bookmark-shaped strips of notebook paper. Have students note the page number next to the word so they can find it again easily when they come to class. Instead of my choosing a list of words to learn, students choose their own. What I'm also trying to demonstrate here is that learning new words is a lifelong process. Though word walls seem like something students remember from elementary school, I ask students to contribute words from their bookmarks to a class list that I collect on a chart. Together we practice using affixes and roots to figure out the words' meaning. If that bears little fruit—for example, with a word like *hubbub*—we turn to context to see if somewhere in the sentence or surrounding paragraph there are clues to the word's meaning. My goal is to demonstrate the habits of mind readers instinctively employ when encountering unfamiliar words.

Students need a robust vocabulary not only to read literature but also to express what they think about what they are reading. For many their thinking, their ability to analyze what they read, is often compromised by the limits of their language. We can help by front-loading key words. These could either be key words important to the central meaning of the text or words that students need in order to talk about the text. Here is an example from the opening of Robert Louis Stevenson's *Treasure Island* as an example. Originally published in 1883, the story was first serialized in the children's magazine *Young Folks*. The influence Stevenson's Long John Silver has had upon our collective imaginations regarding pirates—from Captain Hook in *Peter Pan* to Johnny Depp's portrayal of Jack Sparrow in *The Pirates of the Caribbean*—cannot be overstated. I wanted my seventh graders to understand where the image of a peg-legged captain with a parrot on his shoulder had originated and to be able to discuss the character intelligently.

In *Bringing Words to Life,* Isabel Beck, Margaret McKeown, and Linda Kucan (2002) urge teachers to consider the utility when deciding which words to teach. They recommend focusing on words that are characteristic of mature language users and appear frequently across a variety of domains. These are not necessarily the longest or most unusual words in a text but rather the ones on which students' ability to comprehend hinges. In the opening paragraphs of *Treasure Island* young readers need to know what a *cove* is in order to visualize the location of the Admiral Benbow Inn. They need to know what *grog* is in order to understand why the captain calls the inn a "grog-shop." Beck et al. also recommend teaching words that add precision to students' thinking, words that will help students express themselves with greater specificity. *Gruff, exotic, enigmatic, intimidating,* and *charismatic* can help students describe what they infer in this introduction about Long John Silver's character.

After teaching students these words, I ask them to think of a person or character from a book or movie who could be described as *gruff, exotic, enigmatic, intimidating,* or *charismatic.* I ask students to write for five minutes explaining why they would describe this person in this fashion. Then students turn and share what they have written with a partner, and we listen to a few as a class. I then have students read the opening pages of *Treasure Island* looking for evidence that supports the use of these for describing the captain.

With *sittyated* and *mought,* I urge students to figure out for themselves what the captain means.

Words from the Text

grog

cove

inn

Words to Add Precision to Conceptual Understanding

gruff

exotic

enigmatic

intimidating

charismatic

TREASURE ISLAND BY ROBERT LOUIS STEVENSON

Squire Trelawney, Dr. Livesey, and the rest of these gentlemen having asked me to write down the whole particulars about Treasure Island, from the beginning to the end, keeping nothing back but the bearings of the island, and that only because there is still treasure not yet lifted, I take up my pen in the year of grace 17___ and go back to the time when my father kept the Admiral Benbow inn and the brown old seaman with the sabre cut first took up his lodging under our roof.

I remember him as if it were yesterday, as he came plodding to the inn door, his sea-chest following behind him in a hand-barrow—a tall, strong, heavy, nut-brown man, his tarry pigtail falling over the shoulder of his soiled blue coat, his hands ragged and scarred, with black, broken nails, and the sabre cut across one cheek, a dirty, livid white. I remember him looking round the cover and whistling to himself as he did so, and then breaking out in that old sea-song that he sang so often afterwards: "Fifteen men on the dead man's chest—Yo-ho-ho, and a bottle of rum!" in the high, old tottering voice that seemed to have been tuned and broken at the capstan bars. Then he rapped on the door with a bit of stick like a handspike that he carried, and when my father appeared, called roughly for a glass of rum. This, when it was brought to him, he drank slowly, like a connoisseur, lingering on the taste and still looking about him at the cliffs and up at our signboard.

"This is a handy cove," says he at length; "and a pleasant sittyated grog-shop. Much company, mate?"

My father told him no, very little company, the more was the pity.

"Well, then," said he, "this is the berth for me. Here you, matey," he cried to the man who trundled the barrow; "bring up alongside and help up my chest. I'll stay here a bit," he continued. "I'm a plain man; rum and bacon and eggs is what I want, and that head up there for to watch ships off. What you mought call me? You mought call me captain. Oh, I see what you're at—there"; and he threw down three or four gold pieces on the threshold. "You can tell me when I've worked through that," says he, looking as fierce as a commander.

Mapping Complex Sentence Structures

Did you notice that the first paragraph of *Treasure Island* is all one sentence? Readers young and old find such complex sentences daunting. Instead of ignoring the textual challenge this poses, we address it straight on. I remind students that punctuation is meant to serve as road signs for readers. We peel back the layers of opening phrases to find the core. Together we search for the subject and verb. ("... I take up my pen ... and go back to the time ... "). Suddenly the meaning becomes clear. As Tony remarked, "The guy is just saying he's going to start writing the story!" Indeed he is. Particularly in the opening chapters of any demanding work, students need lots of practice figuring out who is doing what in sentences like Stevenson's. Once readers grasp the elements of a writer's style and the rhythm of the writing in their ears, the difficulty of negotiating such syntax diminishes.

Another method for working with demanding literature is to teach students about theories of reading. Most students have no idea that reading is a much-studied act and that entire schools of thought have been built upon the foundations of this primary skill. Few students have ever given much thought to their reading beyond, "I like to read" or "I don't like to read." In "*You Gotta BE the Book,*" Jeff Wilhelm (1997) describes research that he conducted in his middle school classroom examining the habits of teenage readers. I cannot do justice here to the complexity of Wilhelm's research, but his case studies of three engaged readers point the way to classroom instruction that can help all students become able readers. Wilhelm found that "the response of engaged readers is intensely visual, empathic, and emotional. By focusing in class on the importance of these evocative responses, that is, entering the story world, visualizing people and places, and taking up relationships to characters, less engaged readers were given strategies for experiencing texts and were helped to rethink reading." (144)

> Why do some kids love reading? What is rewarding and engaging about reading for these students? What do these engaged readers "do" as they read that makes the experience fun, satisfying, and engaging for them? Why do other kids hate reading? What in their experience has contributed to their negative view?
>
> I realized that year after year I had encountered students who obviously resisted reading. But they seemed to be a minority, and eventually—I'm ashamed to say—I'd really just given up on them as far as becoming readers was concerned. It was when I encountered a whole class of them that I could not blame them instead of myself, the materials, or the method. Eighth grade remedial reading produced a crisis that required a new way of thinking about and teaching the act of reading. If I wished to pursue my job of developing readers, then resistance and lack of engagement were compelling issues that had to be deeply considered. (7)

Pursuing answers to his questions, Wilhelm experimented with incorporating discussions about reading theory and literary conventions into his lessons. What he found was that as students became increasingly aware of the fact that they were actually going to have to "do" something to make a text comprehensible, their frustrations decreased. Suddenly it wasn't that anything was wrong with them or with the text that was causing them to find a book incomprehensible. They simply weren't doing the things that good readers do when they read. As Umberto Eco (1994) explains, "Every text is a lazy machine asking the reader to do some of the work."

Without diminishing the importance of good early reading instruction or the difficulties that children with disabilities face when reading, I would assert that many "poor readers" are actually lazy readers. This is not a reflection on their character. It's simply that no one ever told these students that reading was going to be hard work. Even when students dutifully skim the assigned pages, few think the homework reading demands from them anything more. Students plug in their iPods, kick back on their beds, and expect the book to transfer information from its pages to their brains. While such a passive stance might work perfectly well for scanning Facebook, it is grossly inadequate for reading Karen Hesse's *Out of the Dust.*

An exchange between two of Wilhelm's students—one an engaged reader, the other a struggling reader—demonstrates how broad the chasm is between students who do and don't know what a text demands of a reader.

John: I can't believe you do all that stuff when you read! Holy crap, I'm not doing . . . like nothing . . . compared to you.

Ron: I can't believe you don't do something. If you don't, you're not reading, man. . . . . It's gotta be like wrestling or watching a movie or playing a video game . . . you've got to like . . . be there! (xiii)

I want students to know that it is not enough simply to cast their eyes over a page of print and expect the story to come alive or even to make sense. A reader needs to act. When reading a book like *A Death in the Family* by James Agee, I have to work very hard to figure out the perspective from which the story is being told. The setting of early-twentieth-century Tennessee is not one I know much about. Agee's gorgeous language can be a distraction from the straightforward business of following the plot. Every sentence seemed imbued with so much meaning that I often lost my way. I had to slow down, check how old particular characters were, and make sure I understood the relationships between characters. Reading a Patricia Cornwall mystery isn't nearly this much work. The payoff is enormous. Whilst I've read a half dozen Kay Scarpetta novels, I can't remember the plot of a single one. *A Death in the Family* is imprinted on my heart.

Louise Rosenblatt (1983) explains:

> The benefits of literature can emerge only from creative activity on the part of the reader himself. He responds to the little black marks on the page, or to the sounds of the words in his head, and he "makes something of the fact." The verbal symbols enable him to draw on his past experiences with what the words point to in life and literature. The text presents these words in a new and unique pattern. Out of these he is enabled actually to mold a new experience, the literary work. (278)

The challenge for any literature teacher is to make these "creative activities" visible to students. Struggling readers often have no idea about the things that expert readers do inside their heads when they read. According to Rosenblatt, good readers conduct a transaction with the text. The reader creates meaning from the words on the page while the text causes the reader to reexamine what he or she knows. The text and the reader interact.

What is so powerful to me about Rosenblatt's work is that she situates the study of literature at the center of every student's life. It is not only the college-bound or future English teachers who need what literature has to offer, but all students. She explains that "literature makes comprehensible the myriad ways in which human beings meet the infinite possibilities that life offers" (6). For most students, for most readers of any age, what is most important is the human experience that literature presents. It is exactly this that drew and continues to draw me to Orhan Pamuk's novels. "The reader seeks to participate in another's vision—to reap knowledge of the world, to fathom the resources of the human spirit, to gain insights that will make his own life more comprehensible" (7). No one has assigned me to read Turkish literature. I read Pamuk because I want to understand more about Istanbul, the crossroad between East and West. His novels don't explain the history of politics of contemporary Istanbul, but they do help me read the news and help me think about the world.

A few years ago I taught a class of extremely reluctant ninth-grade readers. In this small class of twenty, there were seven special education students and five English learners. The four girls in the class staked out their territory in the desks near the door. As I handed out copies of *Romeo and Juliet,* I told the class that this story was going to remind them a lot of people they know and situations they have experienced. We worked our way through the play—acting out scenes, discussing the characters, drawing parallels to teenage life as they knew it. I had students write about arguments they had had with their parents and fights they had witnessed. We studied the formal elements of Shakespeare's play, but only as they functioned in terms of our overall understanding. Feeling and connection had to come first.

Rosenblatt theorizes that literature is a form of personal experience and that as such it "has many potentialities that dynamic and informed teaching may sustain" (222). I interpret her discoveries as follows:

1. Literature fosters the imagination that a healthy democracy requires—the ability to understand the needs and hopes of others and the ability to see how our actions affect other people's lives.

2. Literature offers readers images of behavior and attitudes different from their own.

3. Literature teaches readers about many ways of approaching one's life, including a variety of philosophies upon which to base one's actions and respond to the actions of others.

4. Literature can help readers make sound choices based upon learning from how characters behave at critical moments.

5. Literature invites readers to examine their own personalities and problems objectively.

6. Literature can help to free readers from fears, guilt, and insecurity by offering a broad view of what is commonly seen as "normal."

7. Literature offers outlets for impulses that might otherwise find expression in antisocial behavior.

Many of the students in this ninth-grade class were adept at antisocial behavior. Getting them to sit still for more than ten minutes and to participate in classroom discussion without putting one another down was a daily challenge. But as we made our way through *Romeo and Juliet,* I felt that what Louise Rosenblatt described was occurring before my eyes. Much of their unproductive behavior was a result of their insecurity. As we talked and wrote about how the Montagues and Capulets, as well as well as gangs on campus, behaved toward one another, students seemed to expand their sense of normalcy. José, a bilingual student who has attended several different schools both in Los Angeles and in Puerto Rico over the course of his fourteen years, compared the Prince's final speech with our school principal's rule that anyone involved in a fight will automatically be expelled. Here is the speech from the play:

> Capulet, Montague,
> See what a scourge is laid upon your hate,
> That heaven finds means to kill your joys with love!
> And I, for winking at your discords too,
> Have lost a brace of kinsmen. All are punish'd. (Act 5, scene 3)

And here was our classroom conversation:

José: I don't think the principal's rule is fair because if someone disrespects me I'm not going to let it go, but I guess she doesn't want just to look the other way.

Me: Why do you think that is?

José: Oh, she probably feels responsible when anybody on campus gets hurt, which I don't agree with either, but I think that's just the way she is.

Michelle (the most excitable and outspoken of the four girls in the class): You know Theresa who was in this class the first week? She got kicked out for fighting and sent to Valley [Valley High School]. The principal didn't care who started it. She just expelled everybody.

José: I think she wanted to make an example for other kids. If Mrs. R. says "community" one more time, I think I'm gonna hit somebody.

Me: Don't do that, Roberto. You know it would break her heart to lose another student.

Careless interpretations of Louise Rosenblatt's emphasis on the importance of reader response have led some teachers to abandon the practice of close reading. What is unfortunate about this loss is that student responses, however heartfelt, which are based upon casual or inaccurate reading can lead the reader into confusion rather than to understanding. Teachers need to take time in class to show students how to examine a text in close detail: word by word, sentence by sentence. Ann E. Berthoff (1999) claims that the chief means of teaching critical reading and writing is to "offer students assisted invitations to look and look again at words, sentences, paragraphs." (676). Only then will they develop the skills they need to be powerful readers. Berthoff goes on to explain:

> The disappearance of close reading is not to be confronted with the calm resignation (or secret jubilation?) evinced by those redrawing the boundaries. Without it, as the chief instrument of Practical Criticism, "reader response" is merely personal, merely psychological, merely opinion. The chief value of Practical Criticism is that it is—practical: it is pragmatic. Close reading teaches that the transactions with the text are always tentative and subject to the pragmatic maxim: "If we take it—metaphor, syntax, word, line—this way, what difference would it make to the way we read the rest of the poem? The opus? The age?" Close reading is entailed in critical reading. It is not an elitist, nose-to-the-text, words-on-the-page pedantry but the way of attending to the interplay of saying and meaning. (677)

The kind of close reading that Berthoff describes does not come naturally to teenagers. When explaining what they think about what they have read, most prefer a broad brushstroke rather than a fine line of reasoning. The challenge of the teacher is to help students refine how they examine a piece of literature without destroying their confidence as readers. I start with students' responses but then ask prodding questions that encourage students to return to the text for answers:

- You say you hate the way Odysseus lies to everyone he meets when he returns to Ithaca. Let's look at that scene with Penelope again. What is Odysseus trying to find out with his lies?

- The scene where Odysseus' dog dies of a broken heart upon seeing his master is one of my favorite scenes, too. What does this moment tell you about Odysseus? Read those lines again. What does the state the dog is in suggest about the state of Odysseus' kingdom?

- It is indeed "gross" when all the unfaithful serving maids are hanged. Look at the epic simile Homer uses to describe the scene. "As when either thrushes with their long wings or doves / Rush into a net that has been set in a thicket, / As they come in to roost, and a dreadful bed takes them in; / So they held their heads in a row, and about the necks / Of all there were nooses, that they might die most piteously. / They struggled a little with their feet, but not very long" (Homer 1997, 309). Why do you think Homer compares the serving women to birds?

Teachers need to go beyond encouraging personal responses and push student readers to understand exactly what the author has done with words and sentences, syntax, and diction that elicited such a response in them as readers. Berthoff concludes her essay, which is called "Reclaiming the Active Mind":

> I have been suggesting that close reading and close observations soften and sharpen hard, dull wits (and bright, confident wits) because they offer occasions to enjoy a pleasure in the exercise of the mind. To practice Practical Criticism by rehabilitating looking and looking again and reading slowly—and again—would thus be to reclaim the Imagination, the agency of the active mind. (68)

When the bell rings, I want students to leave class exhausted by how well they have exercised their minds, yet happy about what they have accomplished.

As I reflect upon my own metamorphosis from nonjudgmental facilitator to a more assertive readers' guide, I think that what prompted my development as much as Lisa Delpit's research was the realization that most student readers are nothing like me. When I was growing up I did little else but read. It wasn't a matter of having an unhappy childhood; I simply preferred characters in books to the children down the block for playmates. I read indiscriminately, helter-skelter, with no thought for improving my mind. I believed everyone and everything around me was boring. Everything except for books.

I remember a Christmas day when I was fifteen. Trying to please a most difficult teenager, my godmother had given me a copy of Erich Segal's *Love Story*. I devoured the short novel in the interval between washing dishes and sit-around-the-tree-and-talk-about-how-much-the-babies-had-grown time. I hated the book. And loved hating it. Arrogantly scornful, I remember descending the stairs full of myself and certain that the sentimentality of Segal's story demonstrated beyond a shadow of a doubt the patent intellectual inferiority of my entire family. I hasten to say that I have come to revise this point of view regarding my wonderful and most loving, forgiving, and indulgent family. I have penance done and, like Samuel Taylor Coleridge's Ancient Mariner, "penance more will do." But at fifteen I defined myself against this book chosen by someone who thought she knew me.

When my teachers began assigning classics like *A Tale of Two Cities, The Grapes of Wrath,* and *The Once and Future King,* I was in heaven. I loved the fact that the books were long and that the authors had written lots of other books that

I could read next. I suppose if I had had more friends I might have discovered much earlier that most teenagers didn't share my enthusiasms, but as it was I continued for years with my nose in a book.

When I became a teacher I quickly realized that apart from a few avid readers, most students are unwilling to do the amount of reading that I had taken for granted. I adjusted. But what took me much longer to figure out was just how much help my students needed in order to be able to read demanding books. I had come to these books with broad textual experience and a huge reading vocabulary. I didn't know how much I knew and had no names to put to the things I knew, but in a deep way I understood how stories worked. Few of the students I teach possess what Alfred Tatum calls a reading lineage, a set of books that serve as important markers in their lives. While my students have enormous experience and vast knowledge about a range of things that I was totally ignorant about at their age, including many aspects of life I continue to find baffling, they would have difficulty identifying a chain of texts that have influenced them deeply, that have lead to other books, or that they continue to reread. In *Reading for Their Lives: (Re)Building the Textual Lineages of African American Adolescent Males,* Alfred Tatum (2009) describes his students wearing out a book with rereading when it contains a message they find compelling. His list of forty engaging texts includes *Autobiography of Malcolm X* by Malcolm X and Alex Haley, *Bang* by Sharon Flake, *Black Boy* by Richard Wright, *The Call of the Wild* by Jack London, "The Masque of Red Death" by Edgar Allan Poe, and *Miracle at Monty Middle School,* by Mary A. Monroe. These are the kinds of books I need to put more of into my students' hands.

M. E. Kerr wrote a novel engagingly titled *I'll Love You When You're More Like Me.* Without meaning to, teachers often convey a similar message to students, "We'll teach you when you're more like us." Most teenagers will read exactly as much as is demanded of them. When my own son was sixteen years old, he would think nothing of stopping on page 43 if that was where the homework assignment ended—not even if he knew that the mystery was solved, the gun went off, the girl was saved on page 44. Discouraging? Yes. But as a teacher I need to learn to work with this.

Having a more realistic sense of my students' attitudes toward reading and their need for help when reading demanding texts has made me a better teacher. Does this make me inconsistent for changing my mind about my methods? Not if, according to Thoreau, the "least particle of truth can color our whole life." As long as I live, I intend to keep unlearning and learning anew what I thought before. It's my professional responsibility. It's also my passion.

REDEFINING WHAT WE ASK STUDENTS TO DO

One of the most challenging aspects of assigning a demanding piece of literature is persuading students to do the reading. Though it is possible to find short classic works like Voltaire's *Candide* and Joseph Conrad's *Heart of Darkness* that offer much to sink your teeth into, most novels by Austen, Dickens, Twain, Steinbeck, the Brontës, Dostoevsky, Tolstoy, Cather, Wharton, and Dreiser are more than 300 pages long, a length almost unimaginable to many teenagers. What? Me read that? Consider the novels most often found in schoolbook rooms: *The Old Man in the Sea, The Pearl, Animal Farm,* all of which come in under 200 pages. You would think length was our primary criterion for choosing which books to teach.

Holding Students Accountable for Their Reading

Teachers brave enough to assign long novels often resort to one of two methods for holding students accountable: they punish or they reward. While it is easy to see how draconian punishments discourage reading, rewards can be just as dangerous. Browsing through *Reading Today,* the journal of the International Reading Association, I was startled to discover an article praising an innovative program that paid students for reading books. Have educators lost their minds? Attaching a monetary reward to reading sends kids the message that reading is a painful task, worth doing only if they are compensated. Even more astonishing was the Pizza Hut plan in which students earned free pizzas for completing a certain number of books. The sponsors of the program, people in the business of selling junk food and soft drinks, are doing their best to support education. It is not their fault that the underlying assumption—that children won't read without rewards—is wrong-headed.

Whenever we say, "If you do this, I'll give you that," we devalue *this*. Admittedly every parent alive has resorted to such bribery to cajole children into brushing teeth, putting on socks, and sleeping in their own beds. But by offering the reward of treats for what is simply reasonable behavior, we undermine the satisfaction inherent in completing these tasks for their own sake: healthy teeth, warm feet, rested parents. The same principle holds true for reading demanding literature. By offering extrinsic incentives for completing a novel, we inadvertently send students the message that no one would read this book for pleasure. Rewards may increase the probability that children will accomplish something they don't particularly want to do, but the danger is that the reward ultimately changes the way they do it. Students lose sight of the real reward, what a piece of literature has to offer them, and instead focus on the number of points needed to earn their pizza.

I had been intrigued by Alfie Kohn's book *Punished by Rewards,* but wanted to know more about what he thought about student motivation. So I called him up. The following conversation was published with Kohn's permission in *California English* (1995).

Carol Jago: Alfie, you've written that teachers should stop fiddling with grading systems and get on with the business of helping kids. As a teacher who has spent a lot of time devising point systems that I later discard, I'm intrigued.

Alfie Kohn: Research into grading over recent years yields three conclusions: (i) that it induces less creative thinking, (ii) that it generates less interest in challenging tasks and texts, and (iii) that it diminishes students' interest in learning per se.

CJ: Pretty damning conclusions.

AK: Indeed. The only positive effect of grades tends to be a short-term recall of isolated facts and even that does not hold true for everyone.

CJ: Yet there is the counterargument that without high-stakes grades for a final exam, students tend not to do the reading.

AK: Possibly, but that is a powerful indictment of what the grading system has done to kids' motivation until now, and possibly raises questions about curriculum. Research shows that when the curriculum is engaging and meaningful to students, there is no need to treat them as pets, to reward them with an A for doing what they are told with books they otherwise would not want to touch. Obviously it's much easier to resort to grades, as I must confess I used to do. It's more challenging, it takes more courage and skill, to take notice of students' lack of interest and take up the challenge to rethink what we are asking them to do.

CJ: Rhetoric in the current political climate suggests that if we would just teach what used to be taught in school, everything will be fine.

AK: Yes. The traditional approach that secondary teachers have absorbed is the transmission view of education—cram them full of facts and skills that they can spit up on demand. This is inconsistent with the theory and research about how people learn. Many teachers are familiar with the idea of constructivism that says people of all ages are active meaning makers, creating theories about themselves, the world, and the books they read, and that it is the teacher's job to facilitate that encounter. If you take that seriously, out go the multiple-choice tests along with the grades necessary to enforce them because they grow out of an antiquated set of assumptions about learning. There is a role for assessment: at some point we need to check in with students to get a sense of how well they're doing, how we can help them to learn more effectively next week. But before we look at assessment, we need to ask the more important question—why we want to assess students' work. If we're doing it to "motivate" them, there is a huge collection of evidence showing that this will be ineffective and counterproductive. When you reward people for doing something, as with an A, they tend to become less interested in what they were rewarded for doing. There is a huge amount of research that demonstrates the more you get students to focus on *how* they're doing, the less they're interested in *what* they're doing.

CJ: You have suggested that, in designing curriculum, teachers should apply a ten-year rule. What do you mean?

AK: Before a teacher, especially a middle school or high school instructor, sits down to plan a course, he or she should ask the question, "What can I reasonably expect that students will retain from this course after a decade?" I know that if I'd been asked that question when I was teaching in high school and college, I would have found it profoundly unsettling, because I knew well, or would have known if I had been brave enough to face the question head-on, that all they would have left was a fact here, a stray theory there, a disconnected assumption or a passage from a book. That should lead us to ask what it is we're doing.

CJ: What do you say to people who think that without grades students won't work as hard?

AK: To some extent that's true. It's an indictment of what grades have done to motivation, and it may be an indication of what's going on in that classroom. The last thing we want to do to a student whose interest and curiosity have been eroded by a stick and carrot approach is to offer more sticks and carrots. Better to challenge the myth that there is a single entity called "motivation" that kids can have more or less of. The truth is that there are different kinds of motivation and they are not equal, not equivalent. I always ask groups of teachers I address how many of them understand the difference between extrinsic and intrinsic motivation. Almost every hand goes up, but this doesn't transfer itself to the classroom. It's not just that intrinsic motivation is better; it's undermined by the use of extrinsic motivators. The problem is that it takes more effort to tap intrinsic interest than to say, "Listen up, folks, this is going to be on the test."

I came away from this conversation both encouraged and depressed. His description of intrinsic motivation was congruent with my own experience as a reader. I love keeping a running list on my computer of the books I have read and have done so assiduously since July 2005. I feel proud when I scan that list of 536 titles and use it often when contemplating new books to recommend to students. I also occasionally display it to the class when complaints about summer or holiday reading assignments are expressed. While I agree theoretically with everything Alfie Kohn says here, my daily contact with real teenagers reinforces my certainty that students need to be held accountable for their reading. The compromise I have struck has been to abandon quizzes that ask for simple recall of relatively unimportant detail. For example, "Where did Raskolnikov hide the little boxes and jewelry he stole from the pawnbroker?" Instead I select a key sentence or two from toward the end of the chapter that has been assigned and ask students to write for five minutes, placing this sentence within the context of the story. In the case of Part 2, Chapter 2 in *Crime and Punishment,* I gave a group of seniors the following assignment:

> Explain the following quotation from last night's homework. What is Raskolnikov talking about? What is bothering him? "Again an intense, almost unbearable joy overwhelmed him for an instant, as it had in the police office. 'I have buried my tracks!'"

Krishna Devai responded:

Raskolnikov just put the things he stole from the pawnbroker under a rock. He is acting crazy because the horror of the crime he committed is starting to dawn on him though he can't admit this to himself. For a smart guy he seems kind of stupid to me. I mean anyone could have seen him bury that stuff. I don't think he is thinking straight.

Rather than putting students on the spot to remember details, I am asking them to reflect upon how the story is developing. If I choose the quotation carefully, students are unable to do this without having read the chapter. These short responses are also easy to read and evaluate—no small thing when you meet 150 students a day. I don't assign grades to their responses but simply give students credit or no credit for having done their homework. Often teachers invest an extraordinary amount of time constructing quizzes on homework reading, making copies, and correcting them. It's boring work. A more efficient way to check that students are reading and not resorting to SparkNotes is to go to the SparkNotes website, print copies of the paragraph-long summary of the chapter you assigned for homework, and hand this out when students come to class. Then tell students to write down three things that occurred in the chapter you assigned for homework that don't appear in this paragraph. This simple ploy achieves two purposes. One, students now know that you know some of them are resorting to SparkNotes instead of doing the reading for themselves, and two, the quizzes are simple to correct. You need to save your eyes for students' real writing.

Another way to check on students' reading is to ask them to close their eyes and visualize the most powerful image they remember from last night's reading. I then give each one a large piece of paper, tell them to fold it into four rectangles, and hand out boxes of crayons. In the top-left corner I ask students to draw a picture of a powerful image from the chapter. Artistic talent was not required here, only a sincere effort to put something of what was in their mind's eye on paper. In a second box I asked students to put this picture into words. Lucy Brown wrote:

> **Raskolnikov is catching the man who was following him and asks why he is doing so. The man looks Raskolnikov in the face and calls him a murderer. Raskolnikov freezes at the thought that someone knows he killed the two women. He doesn't understand how the man could know and wracks his brain thinking about it. He goes back to his room and drifts off to sleep. He has a dream that he goes to the pawnbroker's home and she is in the corner laughing. He tries to kill her but at every blow the laughter gets louder and louder.**

In the third box I ask students to imagine they are professors of Russian literature lecturing to a college class on the scene they just described. What I am hoping to elicit here is a shift from recounting events to analysis. It was fascinating to note how students' syntax and diction shifted. In this box Jason wrote:

> **Dear students, in this scene Raskolnikov is sent into a world of utter despair. A strange man has just called him a murderer. Raskolnikov knew he had outwitted the suspicious police officers, but suddenly here was a man**

**calling him a murderer to his face. Where has this man come from? From
inside our hero. The stranger tells Raskolnikov what he is—a murderer.**

In the fourth box I invite students to write a poem, create a word collage, follow a stream of consciousness, or in any other way that suited them, respond to
the scene they had drawn. Marisa Gonzalez had been working with the meeting
between Razumikhin (Raskolnikov's friend and foil) and Raskolnikov where
Razumikhin (his name means "reason" in Russian) realizes what his friend has
done. Marisa created in a matter of seven or eight minutes the following poem
using her own words as well as choosing words and phrases from the text and
rearranging them into the shape of a poem:

> It was dark
> They were looking at one another
> In silence
> Burning and intense eyes
> Piercing into his soul
> Into his consciousness
> Something strange
> Some idea, some hint
> Slipped
> Awful, hideous
> "Do you understand now?"

This activity took up most of a class period but accomplished several things
I wanted to achieve. I had a clear picture of which students had and had not
completed the previous night's reading assignment. Students explored a scene
from the novel that they—rather than I—found powerful. They examined this
moment from various perspectives. By prompting students to move quickly from
one box to the next I hoped to keep them from feeling that they were creating
a finished product. I was concerned with exercising their reading minds. The
resulting papers were not things of beauty to post on a bulletin board, but they
were rich with ideas.

What kinds of grades did I assign to these papers? None. I had the information
I need regarding which students had done the homework, and my students knew
I knew. To allow students who hadn't kept up with the reading to contribute,
I asked them to complete the identical steps for an earlier scene in the novel.
The day's lesson was still valuable for them, but they knew that they had been
found out. Despite Alfie Kohn's warnings about internal and external motivation, I think teenagers keep up with their schoolwork better when they know
that their teacher cares enough to check up on them. No matter how tough they
talk, my students mostly feel bad when they let me down. I always give them
another chance to make it up.

Keeping a Record of Student Reading

A point of Kohn's that particularly impressed me was his ten-year rule. I know exactly what I want my students to retain: a love for the things that literature can do to them. It is less important that students are able to recall the minutiae than it is for them to have been moved by a book. While I believe that wide reading is a defining characteristic of a fully developed human being, I don't think this is necessarily determined by the number of books one has read. The extent to which the books that have been read become integrated into students' selves is much more important. My ten-year rule holds true for all students, not only the college-bound, whose linguistic backgrounds make a long-term relationship with literature seem, if not the most natural thing in the world, at least a reasonable goal. I intend that my struggling readers, my English learners, my truculent students should also be affected by literature. Making this happen is without doubt the most challenging task I face professionally. It's also the most important one.

Many teachers in my English department have students keep a log of all the books they read over the course of the year. The lists are kept inside students' writing portfolios and when the folders move from one grade to the next, students can continue their list. I like this addition to a portfolio because it offers evidence of a student's reading history. Wouldn't you love to see a list of all the books you read from the time you were twelve through eighteen? The document also provides concrete evidence for interesting reflective writing on the development of their literacy.

Late in the spring when students often have difficulty focusing on anything other than upcoming summer vacation, I ask them to pull out their reading logs. These lists contain no annotations, only the title, author, and date the book was completed. Inevitably some students have lost their lists, or lost their portfolios, or transferred from another school. To help these students, we take a few minutes to remind one another of the core works that most students read in class. I encourage everyone to add titles that they remember reading but forgot to list. I then put students into groups and offer them the following questions to stimulate their discussion. I remind them that I'm not looking for pat answers but rather for lively conversation. If groups never get past talking about the first question, it most often means that their book chat was a signal success.

- Which of the books on your list would you recommend to an incoming ninth grader as a "must read"?
- Which of these books do you think you might someday reread?
- Are there any books on this list that you find you still think about from time to time?

- Was there a series of books or kinds of books, like fantasy or science fiction, that you got "hooked" on?

- If you had to choose one character from all of these books that you would most like to meet, who would it be?

When I see that the conversations are sputtering, I ask students to write for ten minutes describing how they think they have developed as readers since they first entered middle school. Which books have been milestones for them? Which titles do they feel are part of their personal reading legacy? As readers, where do they plan to go from here?

Even students who have read very little seem to have something to write about, particularly after the group discussions. Many students write about books they expected to hate but later came to enjoy. Some write about books that a classmate just told them about and that they now plan to read. Occasionally students ask if they can write about a book from their childhood like *Harriet the Spy*. How could I say no? Others lament that they know they haven't read as much as they should. Some blame this on lame teachers. More blame themselves. Students always seem responsive to this invitation to look backward and then ahead to their future as readers. Writing about their reading also helps send the message that reading isn't just something one does because an English teacher says you must.

Wayne Booth (1998) wrote, "When teachers are fully successful, they are successful beyond any of their conscious intentions about particular subjects: they make converts, they make souls that have been turned around to face a given way of being and moving in the world" (298). That's what I want to do: make converts. I suppose the fourteen years I spent in Catholic schools may have something to do with this, but I see it as my mission in life to turn students into readers whose way of moving in the world is somehow shaped by literature. I want them to see their own lives as a hero's journey and to have learned from Odysseus and Bilbo Baggins that even when there seems to be no hope for survival, help will appear, though not always in the shape one might expect. I want them to have the courage to put themselves at risk—like Huck Finn and Robin Hood—for the sake of others. I want their experience of reading Elie Wiesel's *Night* to affect them so profoundly that they are never quite the same. My goal is to teach students how to read so well that their hearts beat with Wiesel's as he reexamines his faith. I also want former students to feel vaguely sick when they go for too long without having read a good book. I don't pretend to be fully successful in this endeavor. But the good sisters also taught me about optimism and perseverance. I know that seeds planted in middle school often do not bear fruit until much, much later.

The Power of Stories

Anna in the Tropics, the 2003 Pulitzer Prize–winning play by Nilo Cruz, offers a striking example of the power of stories in a Cuban cigar factory. Following a traditional nineteenth-century practice, the owner has hired a lector to read to his employees as they roll and pack cigars. At the curtain's rise, the old lector has just finished reading *Wuthering Heights.* The new lector arrives with a copy Leo Tolstoy's *Anna Karenina.* The stories do more than provide an imaginative escape from tedious work; they offer a mirror in which the factory workers see their own lives and loves reflected. Anna, Karenin, and Vronsky offer alternate ways of being and feeling. The employees talk about these characters as though they are real.

Robert Scholes (1989) says, "Reading is not just a matter of standing safely outside texts, where their power cannot reach us. It is a matter of entering, of passing through the looking glass and seeing ourselves on the other side" (27). This is what reading does for me. It is what I also want for my students. I experienced what Scholes describes while I was reading Virginia Woolf's *Mrs. Dalloway.* How I managed to earn a degree in English without having read this novel I will never know, but I came to the book these many years later through Michael Cunningham's 1999 Pulitzer Prize–winning novel, *The Hours.* It is a wonderful short novel, well worth reading if you have never read it or only seen the movie with Meryl Streep and Ed Harris.

One of the three intertwined stories in *The Hours* is a biographically accurate account of Virginia Woolf's life while she wrote *Mrs. Dalloway.* As soon as I finished Cunningham's final page, I could not rest until I had read *Mrs. Dalloway.* I was indulging in one of my periodic reading binges, moving from book to book with frenetic urgency. Reading Mrs. Dalloway's musings, I passed through what Scholes describes as the looking glass of Woolf's text and found myself on the other side. For all the obvious differences of time, place, and dress, Clarissa and I have a lot in common. We are both creatures of enormous habit, making a virtue of these habits even when others view them as eccentricities. We both focus on details, even when this sometimes means missing the bigger picture. We both know how to throw a wonderful party.

Now, I am sure any Woolf scholar who might happen to read what I have just written is likely to be thinking, "What rubbish. Who cares about such personal drivel?" Well, readers care. Robert Scholes explains, "Reading is always, at once, the effort to comprehend and the effort to incorporate" (9). Readers (or listeners in the case of *Anna in the Tropics*) are constantly engaged in both understanding the text and in connecting to it. One without the other is an incomplete reading. Ten years from now this is the kind of reader I want my students to be. I want them to go on reading binges and know the feeling of needing a book (or a lector) as urgently as a thirsty man needs water. I want them to have the reading skills they need to negotiate any text, classic or contemporary. I want them to know what it feels like to step through the looking glass and see themselves in the characters they meet.

Inevitably, the day comes when the student must read or choose not to read without the lure of a grade or free pizza. My job as a literature teacher is to develop independence rather than dependence. I don't know a single teacher who makes house calls to former students struggling with a metaphor. They must learn to do it for themselves.

Identifying Nonfiction Works for the Curriculum

It's hard to be an effective proponent of the reading habit without being a reader yourself. As Will Rogers once said, "You can't teach what you don't know any more than you can come back from where you ain't been." If there is one area where many English teachers often have a blind spot, it is with nonfiction. So many of us are avid readers of fiction that we don't have nonfiction titles on the tip of our tongues the way we should. One of the most frequent concerns I hear about the Common Core is its recommendation that students need to read many more informational texts. There is no need to panic. There is a plethora of outstanding nonfiction for young readers. Here are a few titles my students have found compelling:

Nonfiction for Readers in Grades 6–8

Every Bone Tells a Story, Jill Rubalcaba and Peter Robertshaw

Chasing Lincoln's Killer, James L. Swanson

The Dark Game: True Spy Stories, Paul Janeczko

Getting Away with Murder, Chris Crowe

Through My Eyes, Ruby Bridges

An American Plague: The True and Terrifying Story of the Yellow Fever Epidemic of 1793, Jim Murphy (a wonderful book to pair with Laurie Halse Anderson's novel *Fever 1793*)

Black Potatoes: The Story of the Great Irish Famine 1845–1850, Susan Campbell Bartoletti

Becoming Billie Holiday, Carole Weatherford

The Greatest: The Story of Muhammad Ali, Walter Dean Myers

The Translator, Daoud Hari

Boy, Tales of Childhood, Roald Dahl

A Dangerous Engine: Benjamin Franklin from Scientist to Diplomat, Joan Dash

In Defiance of Hitler: The Secret Mission of Varian Fry, Carla Killough McClafferty

The Wall: Growing Up Behind the Iron Curtain, Peter Sis

The Longitude Prize, Joan Dash

Dreams from My Father, Barack Obama

The History of Us, Joy Hakim

Nonfiction for Readers in Grades 9–10

Long Way Gone: Memoir of a Boy Soldier, Ishmael Beah

Cod: The Biography of the Fish That Changed the World, Mark Kurlansky

Stiff: The Curious Lives of Human Cadavers, Mary Roach

Food Rules, Michael Pollan

Anatomy of a Face, Lucy Greely

Zeitoun, Dave Eggers

Enrique's Journey, Sonia Nazario

Into the Wild, Jon Krakauer

Mountains Beyond Mountains, Tracy Kidder

Animals in Translation, Temple Grandin

Tipping Point, Malcolm Gladwell

Profiles in Courage, John F. Kennedy

President Reagan: The Role of a Lifetime, Lou Cannon

The Lexus and the Olive Tree, Thomas Friedman

The Wrecking Crew, Thomas Frank

Long Walk to Freedom: The Autobiography of Nelson Mandela, Nelson Mandela

Mornings on Horseback, David McCullough

Washington's Crossing, David Hackett Fischer

Nonfiction for Readers in Grades 11–12

Blood Done Sign My Name, Timothy Tyson

Columbine, Dave Cullen

Nickel and Dimed, Barbara Ehrenreich

The Botany of Desire, Michael Pollan

Methland: The Death and Life of an American Small Town, Nick Reding

The Immortal Life of Henrietta Lacks, Rebecca Skloot

The Forever War, Dexter Filkins

The Man Who Mistook His Wife for a Hat by Oliver Sacks

Justice: What's the Right Thing to Do? Michael J. Sandel

Team of Rivals: The Political Genius of Abraham Lincoln, Doris Kearns Goodwin

America in Our Time: From World War II to Nixon, Godfrey Hodgson

Wealth and Power in America, Gabriel Kolko

The Cash Nexus: Money and Power in the Modern World, Niall Ferguson

Essence of Decision: Explaining the Cuban Missile Crisis, Graham T. Allison

Kennedy, Theodore C. Sorensen

The Grand Chessboard, Zbigniew Brzezinski

The Nuclear Delusion, George Kennan

Vietnam: A History, Stanley Karnow

Battle Cry of Freedom, James McPherson

The Path Between the Seas, David McCullough

I want students to read nonfiction not only because it accords with Common Core Standards, but because they need to read history, science, and psychology in order to know more about the world around them.

5

In those days folk still believed in witches and trembled at a curse; and this one, falling so pat, like a wayside omen, to arrest me ere I carried out my purpose, took the pith out of my legs.

— Robert Louis Stevenson, KIDNAPPED

READING LITERATURE FOR COMMON UNDERSTANDING

Reading literature helps students acquire greater awareness of their own and other cultures. It can stimulate intellectual curiosity about the sociological, historical, political, artistic, religious, and psychological *mores* of cultures portrayed in the books we teach. Rich literature allows students to appreciate the universality of human experience across the centuries and around the globe. Such reading entails work, but this work should be encouraged rather than avoided. Children are shortchanged when their teachers shy away from difficult books.

A study conducted by ACT called "Reading Between the Lines" found that the students who were most likely to be successful in post-secondary educational settings were those who could comprehend complex texts. The report defines a complex text as one that "contains multiple layers of meaning not all of which will be immediately apparent to students on a single superficial reading" (2006) and describes six key features of such text:

1. *Relationships*: Interactions among ideas or characters in the text are subtle, involved, or deeply embedded.

2. *Richness:* The text possesses a sizable amount of highly sophisticated information conveyed through data or literary devices.

3. *Structure:* The text is organized in ways that are elaborate and sometimes unconventional.

4. *Style*: The author's tone and use of language are often intricate.

5. *Vocabulary:* The author's choice of words is demanding and highly context dependent.

66

6. *Purpose*: The author's intent in writing the text is implicit and sometimes ambiguous.

The Common Core initiative employed this ACT research as its starting point for developing standards that require students to read complex texts. "The ACT report is one part of an extensive body of research attesting to the importance of text complexity in reading achievement. The clear, alarming picture that emerges from the evidence is that while the reading demands of college, workforce training programs, and citizenship have held steady or risen over the past fifty years, K–12 texts have, if anything, become less demanding. This finding is the impetus behind the Standards' strong emphasis on increasing text complexity as a key requirement in reading" (2010). In Appendix A, the Common Core document describes text complexity both qualitatively—the aspects of a text that can be determined only by a human reader, such as purpose, clarity, and the demands of background knowledge—and quantitatively—the aspects of a text that can be measured mechanically such as word frequency, sentence length, and text cohesion. The authors recommend that teachers take into consideration additional variables such as student motivation and prior experience when selecting texts for the curriculum.

The Common Core Standards struck a compromise between those who lobbied for a national grade-by-grade reading list and those who felt the choice of texts should remain in local hands. Appendix B of the online document includes a list of text exemplars for grades K–12. The stories, poetry, drama, and nonfiction listed are meant to "exemplify the level of complexity and quality that the Standards require all students in a given grade band to engage with. Additionally, they are suggestive of the breadth of texts that students should encounter in the text types required by the Standards. The choices should serve as useful guideposts in helping educators select texts of similar complexity, quality, and range for their own classrooms." Given the concern expressed by many that this list would indeed become the national curriculum, it is important to note and repeat to anyone who insists otherwise. "They expressly do not represent a partial or complete reading list" (2).

Are publishers likely to include these texts in revisions to language arts textbooks? Of course they will. But anyone who portrays the texts on these lists as mandated reading is misinterpreting the document's intention. An individually designed curriculum in which students read literary works of comparable quality, complexity, and range is aligned to the Common Core. Teach literature you love, and your students will be more likely to love it, too.

Lest you think the impetus for teaching complex texts is some new-fangled notion, see what the introduction of the 1901 Ginn & Company sixth-grade literature book has to say about the importance of reading literature:

> Literature in its noblest form should do for the child what it does for the man—open the eyes to clearer vision, and nourish and inspire the soul.

The reading book, therefore, has more direct influence upon the character of the pupil than any other text-book, and, with this in mind, it has been the fundamental purpose of this series to make its readers familiar with the best writers and their works. (Cyr 1901, 3)

Given the influence of the "reading book" on the character of the pupil, it worries me to see the direction in which many textbook publishers are heading. Rather than focusing on "the best writers and their works," they seem to be searching for the perfect language arts video game to sell to schools. In an attempt to transition to the digital age, publishers are keen to offer a dazzling array of materials with flashy page design, gorgeous artwork, and lots of high-tech "apps." It is easy to see why they and their textbook products are moving in this direction. By the age of twenty-one, the average gamer will have spent 10,000 hours playing video games, approximately the same amount of time spent in school from grades 5–12. Game designer Jane McGonigal from the Institute of the Future thinks this is a good idea. She argues that gamers are caught up in endeavors they find blissfully productive. Many of today's young people feel they can be their best selves in the virtual word. Imagine if students put a comparable amount of effort into reading and writing that they do into *World of Warcraft*. Imagine if students felt so "blissfully productive" at the end of every school day that they were eager to return on the morrow for more.

We are seeing a mass exodus of young people from the real world to virtual worlds. I am concerned that their blissful engagement in virtual worlds could lead to a dangerous disengagement from the real. In Aldous Huxley's *Brave New World,* the masses went to the feelies and took *soma* to keep them from thinking too much about problems in their society and in their lives. If we care only about keeping kids satisfied with their lot as Deltas, turning language arts textbooks into giant online games may be an excellent plan. If, on the other hand, we believe that our mission as teachers is to prepare students for life in the real world, teaching literature seems to be a much superior one. This doesn't mean we can't learn from and capitalize on what students find so compelling about online games. Why not integrate some of the positive aspects of video gaming into literature lessons? For example:

1. Allow students many opportunities to fail. Gamers die a thousand times before achieving an epic win. In the same manner, readers need multiple, no-stakes chances to practice the same skill over and over until the action becomes automatic.

2. Offer feedback on student work as soon and as often as possible. This allows students to adjust their performance continuously and as a result of the feedback to "level up."

COMMON CORE TEXT EXEMPLARS

Grades 6–8

Stories

Little Women, Louisa May Alcott
The Adventures of Tom Sawyer, Mark Twain
A Wrinkle in Time, Madeleine L'Engle
The Dark Is Rising, Susan Cooper
Dragonwings, Laurence Yep
Roll of Thunder, Hear My Cry, Mildred D. Taylor
"The People Could Fly," Virginia Hamilton
The Tale of the Mandarin Ducks, Katherine Paterson
"Eleven," Sandra Cisneros
Black Ships Before Troy: The Story of The Iliad, Rosemary Sutcliff

Drama

Sorry, Wrong Number, Lucille Fletcher
The Diary of Anne Frank: A Play, Frances Goodrich and Albert Hackett

Grades 9–10

Stories

The Odyssey, Homer
Metamorphoses, Ovid
"The Nose," Nikolai Gogol
Candide, Or The Optimist, Voltaire
Fathers and Sons, Ivan Turgenev
"The Gift of the Magi," O. Henry
The Metamorphosis, Franz Kafka
The Grapes of Wrath, John Steinbeck
Fahrenheit 451, Ray Bradbury
"I Stand Here Ironing," Tillie Olsen
Things Fall Apart, Chinua Achebe
To Kill a Mockingbird, Harper Lee
The Killer Angels, Michael Shaara
The Joy Luck Club, Amy Tan
In the Time of the Butterflies, Julia Álvarez
The Book Thief, Marcus Zusak

Drama

Oedipus the King, Sophocles
The Tragedy of Macbeth, William Shakespeare
A Doll's House, Henrik Ibsen
The Glass Menagerie, Tennessee Williams
Rhinoceros, Eugene Ionesco
"Master Harold". . . and the Boys, Athol Fugard

Grades 11–12

Stories

The Canterbury Tales, Geoffrey Chaucer
Don Quixote, Miguel de Cervantes
Pride and Prejudice, Jane Austen
"The Cask of Amontillado," Edgar Allan Poe
Jane Eyre, Charlotte Brontë
The Scarlet Letter, Nathaniel Hawthorne
"A White Heron," Sarah Orne Jewett
Billy Budd, Sailor, Herman Melville
"Home," Anton Chekhov
The Great Gatsby, F. Scott Fitzgerald
As I Lay Dying, William Faulkner
A Farewell to Arms, Ernest Hemingway
Their Eyes Were Watching God, Zora Neale Hurston
"The Garden of Forking Paths," Jorge Luis Borges
The Adventures of Augie March, Saul Bellow
The Bluest Eye, Toni Morrison
Dreaming in Cuban, Cristina Garcia
The Namesake, Jhumpa Lahiri

Drama

The Tragedy of Hamlet, William Shakespeare
Tartuffe, Jean-Baptiste Molière
The Importance of Being Earnest, Oscar Wilde
Our Town: A Play in Three Acts, Thornton Wilder
Death of a Salesman, Arthur Miller
A Raisin in the Sun, Lorraine Hansberry
Death and the King's Horseman: A Play, Wole Soyinka

3. Invite students to devise solutions to textual problems independently and creatively. Gamers know to open every box and knock on every door. Too many readers look to the teacher for help only when they are in trouble.

4. Encourage collaboration. Though gaming may look like a solitary pastime, teamwork and competition contribute enormously to players' engagement. Create tasks that require students to work together in order to achieve the lesson's goal.

The purposes of a good literature textbook and a powerful literature curriculum have not changed much since 1901. The Ginn & Company reader sought to awaken interest in students in the world around them along with a deepening their understanding of their own experience.

> We have been reading and becoming acquainted with the American poets; now we enter a new field of literature, and the great prose writers, Hawthorne, Irving, Dickens, and Scott, with the English poet Tennyson, shed the influence of their characters and writings in the schoolroom. The pupil looks into their faces and visits their homes. Their early childhood, their battles with adversity, and the influences that determined the current of their lives become familiar. Then, with awakened interest and admiration, he reads the messages they have left behind them. (4)

Over one hundred years later, I want my students to do the same. I want to help them figure out how to make this a better, not an alternate universe.

Working in the Zone of Proximal Development

It is interesting to note that the challenge of matching the student's reading ability and maturity with the text was no less a concern in 1901 than it is now for teachers selecting texts that match the quality, complexity, and richness of those on the Common Core list. "Characteristic selections from these authors have been carefully chosen with reference to the capacity of the children" (4). Long before Lev Vygotsky (1962) formulated his zone of proximal development, educators and textbook publishers were weighing the merits of literary texts against students' development as readers. Vygotsky believed that teachers should design instruction that challenges students to stretch. If lessons include only work that students can accomplish without the help of their teacher, they are being shortchanged. The effective teacher aims instruction just beyond what students are able to perform independently.

> What the child can do in cooperation today he can do alone tomorrow. Therefore the only good kind of instruction is that which marches ahead of development and leads it; it must be aimed not so much at the ripe as at the ripening functions. (104)

In too many classrooms, instruction is marching behind development; I believe we underestimate our students' capacity for comprehending literature. Persuaded by teenage complaints, we assign an author's shorter novel regardless of its relative merit against a longer work or a short story instead of a novel at all. Giving in to students' moans—which to my mind are developmentally appropriate—we substitute easy-to-read books for serious literature.

This is not to say that there isn't a place for light reading in everyone's life. I would be lost without my occasional fix from Daniel Silva and Carl Hiaasen. But these are not the kind of texts that deserve the close scrutiny and probing discussions that a rigorous literature class is designed to promote. What I suggest as a solution to the dilemma of needing time for recreational reading within the school day as well as time for instruction and discussion is to have every student in middle and high school enrolled in two periods of English. One period would be reserved for reading and the other, what we now consider their English class. Both would carry credit. In the reading class students would be free to choose any book they like—this could be the text they have been assigned for homework in their English class or the latest Gary Paulsen novel—and to read for fifty uninterrupted minutes. Students would never have to write a book report about what they read. Once a week, students might talk with one another about books that they have enjoyed, but their reading would be otherwise undisturbed.

I am not unaware of the difficulty of rearranging a school's master schedule or of the additional cost involved in such a plan, but the benefits would be enormous. English teachers would meet half as many students in a day. For thirty-five years the National Council of Teachers of English has recommended that English teachers should meet no more than eighty students in a day. In California, budget cuts have resulted in many middle and high school teachers meeting up to 200 students on any school day. In Florida, teachers are assigned six 45-minute periods of instruction. Under such conditions, it isn't possible to teach as well as we know how. Pragmatist that I am, I know that the current schedule at my school is unlikely to change. I have fifty-five minutes a day with my students. This works out to 275 instructional minutes a week. For most classes I set aside seventy-five of these minutes weekly for reading. I don't carve out one day or the first fifteen minutes of every day for reading, but rather intersperse the reading time as needed within my lesson plans.

For example, when I think that students will find a chapter particularly difficult, I ask them to read a page and then we talk about what we have read together. After a few minutes of discussion, we read another two pages. We talk some more. With each break, I extend the length of the passage to be read. This is a far from foolproof system because the slowest readers have trouble keeping up, whatever pace I set, but if I am sensitive about not putting these students on the spot to respond to what they haven't yet read, students tell me that the exercise helps them keep reading. I wish I could simply assign thirty pages for homework and that every student would return the next day with the task completed. I am not making excuses for them, but many of my students' home lives preclude such a commitment to schoolwork. I have found that the more intentional I am about attaching their homework to class work, the more likely the work is to get done. And the more attentive I am to these special needs, the more successful I am in helping my students open their "eyes to clearer vision" and read the kinds of books that will "nourish and inspire the soul."

Is the Printed Word as Dead as Rosencrantz and Guildenstern?

Teachers in the United States are not alone in their struggle to maintain a literature-rich curriculum. Speaking to a group of British English teachers taking part in an institute to rediscover their love of literature, playwright Tom Stoppard lamented the decline of the printed page in education. "The printed word is no longer in as demand as it was when I was at the age of pupils or even at the age of the teachers teaching them. The moving image is taking precedence in children's lives over the printed page" (Jones 2010). The author of *Rosencrantz and Guildenstern Are Dead* does not want "the printed word to be swept away." Neither do I. Whether words come to us on paper or screen is not the issue. The link to this article on the *Guardian* website was forwarded to me by a friend via

"Unless you are educated in metaphor, you are not safe to be let loose in the world."
—*Robert Frost*

email! I love the access to information the Internet affords. Stoppard, a modern master of wordplay, worries that for children today the printed word is losing value. English teachers may be the last best chance for keeping the printed word alive.

A national survey conducted by Sandra Stotsky (2010) and supported by the National Endowment for the Humanities on literary study in grades 9–11 found:

> First, the content of the literature and reading curriculum for students in standard or honors courses is no longer traditional or uniform in any consistent way. The most frequently mentioned titles are assigned in only a small percentage of courses, and the low frequencies for almost all the other titles English teachers assign point to an idiosyncratic literature curriculum for most students. Moreover, the works teachers assign do not increase in difficulty from grade 9 to grade 11.
>
> Second, teachers of standard and honors courses do not regularly engage students in close, analytical reading of assigned works. They do draw on a variety of approaches for literary study, including close reading, but they are more likely to use a non-analytical approach to interpret a work (e.g., a personal response or a focus on a work's historical, cultural, or biographical context) than to undertake a careful analysis of the work itself. It is not clear why English teachers favor non-analytical approaches. Nevertheless, an under-use of analytical reading to understand non-fiction and a stress on personal experience or historical context to understand either an imaginative or a non-fiction text may be contributing to the high remediation rates in post-secondary English and reading courses. (2010)

The Common Core Standards represent one attempt to address both the complexity of the literature assigned in English classrooms as well as the complexity of the work—the thinking and analysis—students are expected to do once they have read the text. How this will play out in the reading lives of students depends on their teachers and particularly their teachers' ability to make the work intellectually engaging.

Shortchanged by Excerpts

Another way in which I believe that instruction is falling behind students' zone of proximal development is in the use of short excerpts to stand in for a writer's body of work. When textbook publishers began including more multicultural literature in their anthologies, they were faced with a dilemma. How to include more authors without making the books too heavy for students to carry? Their solution was to resort to excerpts from the big names they knew they had to include and short poems from multicultural authors. Longer poems, drama, and stories from outstanding contemporary writers like Ana Castillo, John Edgar

Wideman, Junot Díaz, August Wilson, Denise Chavez, Alice Walker, and Victor Hernández Cruz often posed problems for adoption on account of their use of offensive language and sexual references. The table of contents looked both traditionally classic as well as diverse, but too often, the quality and comprehensibility of the literature students were reading suffered. I saw this for myself when I attempted to teach Thoreau from a literature anthology.

One afternoon a colleague of mine had to leave school at the spur of the moment and asked me to teach her American Literature class. I readily agreed and asked what they were reading. She said, "Thoreau" and dashed for the door. "Wonderful," I thought. I love Thoreau and hadn't reread him for years. This afternoon was going to be fun. Well, it would have been if we had had before us anything that remotely resembled Thoreau's writings. Instead of a coherent extended excerpt, the anthology that students were reading from offered snippets of Thoreau under headings link: "Solitude," "Nature," "Work." How could we discuss Thoreau's challenging ideas with only aphorisms to work from? I tried asking the discussion questions that followed each passage, but gave up when I couldn't figure out the answers either. There simply wasn't enough text to go on. I told the students to close their books and allow me to read to them from a copy of *Civil Disobedience* that I had fortunately brought along. One student asked me if all the things they were reading in their textbook came from "real books like that." I wanted to cry. Thoreau Lite is worse than no Thoreau at all.

I recognize that for many schools and for many teachers literature anthologies make both economic and educational sense. New teachers should not be expected to construct a course in American literature from whole cloth. Literature anthologies also provide teachers with valuable background information on authors and offer good suggestions for extended readings. My complaint is with the selections themselves. I hate excerpts. One anthology that shall remain nameless actually published only the first third of a play. Why would anyone who cares about literature do such a thing? Did they expect that students would go out and buy a copy of the play to find out what happens to the characters next? I know I am ranting here, but it seems essential that works of literature should not be carved up, even given the limitations of a student's available reading time and the number of pages available in the volume. It will be interesting to see if web-based textbooks will include more whole works of literature given that the cost of ink and paper and the sheer weight of the anthologies are no longer issues.

I don't just want my students to know who Thoreau is in order to be able to identify him correctly on a cultural literacy quiz; I want them to spend time at Walden Pond and drink deeply of Thoreau's ideas. In the 1901 Ginn reader, "These selections have been somewhat abridged, but it has been thought wiser to have them a little longer than many text-books introduce, rather than to mar the symmetry and beauty of the author's work" (Cyr 1901, 4). Now there was a publishing company that knew what it was doing.

Literary Allusions in Contemporary Discourse

Along with opening up geographically and historically unfamiliar worlds to students, reading literature can also serve as a key to unlocking the doors of meaning to many references in the world that surrounds them. Bloggers, newspaper editors, journalists, and cartoonists take pleasure employing literary allusions in their writing. It's like a secret language, one that only readers speak. When students ask me why they need to read Edith Hamilton's *Mythology* or stories from the Bible, I tell them facetiously that it is so they can understand *The New Yorker* cartoons. Never having seen a copy of the magazine and unable to imagine why they would ever choose to, students look at me as though I have finally, truly lost my mind.

For years I have, with the help of students, collected cartoons with literary references. One of my favorites was the February 17, 1997, cover of *The New Yorker* in which a love-struck monster stands by with flowers and valentine in hand as Victor Frankenstein prepares to throw the switch and bring to life an obviously female creature. I ask students to ponder how bereft they would be without the background information necessary to "read" this cover illustration. The clever ones remind me that Victor Frankenstein refused to create a girlfriend for the monster.

Throughout the school year I offer students extra credit for every literary reference they find in the news or elsewhere in public discourse. One student brought in a cell phone ad with the screen message: "CAESAR—KEEP YOUR EYE ON BRUTUS—WILL EXPLAIN LATER." We talked about whether Artemidorus might have used such a means to communicate with Caesar had the technology been available in ancient Rome. During the Bill Clinton impeachment proceedings, another student found a Paul Conrad political cartoon in which Kenneth Starr and President Clinton are robed in Roman dress. A bloody body lies on the steps of the Capitol while a toga-clad elephant peeks from behind a column with a dripping dagger in its trunk. When George Stephanopoulos' exposé of the Clinton White House was published, a *Los Angeles Times* headline read, "Stephanopoulos Tells All; Critics Ask: Et Tu, George?"

My purpose in urging students to search for such classical references is to draw attention to their ubiquitous presence in contemporary discourse. I explain that writers and cartoonists use classical references as shorthand to comment on current conditions and public figures. Editors count on the fact that their readers will have had some experience with certain well-known books and have at least a vague memory of them. A cover of *The New York Times Magazine* carried a picture of two babies, one a boy, the other a girl and the caption, "It's a . . . (your choice). A new sperm-splitting machine lets couples select a child's sex. All's well or Orwell?" The reference here is, of course, to George Orwell's *1984.* My students were quick to point out that a better choice would have been Aldous Huxley's *Brave New World,* where genetic engineering was the norm. I replied that my guess is that Orwell's name has come to be synonomous with a dangerously dehumanizing future—and that it was easier to rhyme with than Huxley.

In the opening gambit of a June 21, 2010, op-ed piece, David Brooks borrows from the legend of Faust to describe the political landscape:

> It was the winter of 2007. Dr. Faustus, the famous left-wing philologist, was sitting in a coffee shop in despair over the Bush–Cheney regime and the future of his country.
>
> Suddenly, Mephistopheles, who happened to be the provost at his college, appeared, sipping a double mocha frappuccino. He sat down next to Dr. Faustus and casually asked him if he would like to be granted any five wishes in exchange for his immortal soul.
>
> This was Dr. Faustus' chance to do something grand for his country. He would lose his soul, but if he chose wisely, he could make the United States a bastion of liberalism forevermore.
>
> "I agree, Lord of Darkness, if you grant me the following wishes: First, I would like the nation to be hurled into an economic crisis caused by Wall Street greed and recklessness. This will discredit free-market fundamentalism once and for all."
>
> "It will be done," Mephistopheles vowed.

Examples of literary references in everyday discourse demonstrate that it is not only bespectacled English teachers who know these books and characters but most educated people. I posted several cartoons and advertisements with literary allusions on a bulletin board and asked a group of tenth graders who had recently read *Julius Caesar* what they thought.

Reed: I admit it's cute what that cell phone ad did, but isn't it really elitist? I mean, what if somebody never read *Julius Caesar* in school? Or what if they were absent that week?

Bryan: Then they don't get the joke. I saw another one by that company that used *The Wizard of Oz*. Maybe the person looking at that version of the ad watches movies. Advertisers just want to grab your attention.

Me: That's a good point. Advertisers use references to connect their product to buyers. If one reference doesn't catch them, maybe another will. But why do you think the political caroonist decided to cast Kenneth Starr and President Clinton as Antony and Caesar?

Bryan: He's being really clever because he changes only two words in Antony's line, but it makes all the difference. Antony opens his funeral oration with, "Friends, Romans, Countrymen, lend me your ears. / I come to bury Caesar, not to praise him." The cartoonist has Starr saying, "I come to bury Clinton, not to censure him."

Lisa: I think Conrad wanted to make that same point Shakespeare made about Antony pretending to the people that he was only acting as a friend and not in fact trying to stir them up against the conspirators. Ken Starr pretends to be all official and without a personal axe to grind when really—

Bryan: Exactly! Antony praises Caesar and Starr censures Clinton. Sorry, Lisa.

Lisa: What I was going to say was that Antony pretends to praise Brutus and Cassius by calling them "honourable men," but really he praises Caesar and makes Brutus and Cassius out to be murderers.

Reed: But if you never read the play, the cartoon makes no sense. I mean, it makes us all feel smart because we see what the cartoonist is doing, but what about everybody else?

Bryan: Well, maybe they should read the play.

Reed: You're a snob, Bryan.

Me: What about Reed's point? What do you think, Anna?

Anna: I think the cartoonist is trying to say something that is really complicated and that referring to *Julius Caesar* makes it easier for him to communicate what he wants to say. He thinks that the Republicans have stabbed Clinton in the back and that Starr really is out to bury the president. Can I show you this other cartoon I found?

Me: Of course. (The political cartoon, again by Paul Conrad, depicts a hand holding a skull with a bullet in it. The caption takes Hamlet's line, "Alas poor Yorick! I knew him, Horatio" and substitues Kosovo for Yorick.)

Anna: I didn't understand it, but I am really upset about what is going on in Kosovo so I asked my older brother what it meant.

Me: Don't tell me, your brother is reading *Hamlet*.

Anna: Yes, but I guess I want to support what Reed was saying because that cartoon really made no sense at all to me, and even after my brother explained about the gravedigger, I still didn't exactly understand. Maybe I will after I read the play in twelfth grade.

Conversations like these help students begin to see that there is something enduring in the stories of Mary Shelley and William Shakespeare that writers and artists continue to draw from. I encourage students to argue about the potential elitism of literary references. I also want them to get the jokes. Over time I hope they will develop an awareness of the enduring things literature has to offer them. For all our progress and technological prowess, it's still hard to say it better than Shakespeare. Literature also allows journalists like David Brooks to frame their subject within a larger context and thereby lend greater significance to their messages. In an essay critiquing the absence of African American characters in the fall television lineup of programs, Howard Rosenberg (1999) makes reference to Ralph Ellison's *Invisible Man.*

> "I am an invisible man," says the African American narrator in one of this country's great novels, the one about a man whose black form fades into the darkness of the coal cellar where he lives. The hero of Ralph Ellison's *Invisible Man* goes on: "No, I am not a spook like those who haunted Edgar Allan Poe; nor am I one of your Hollywood-movie ectoplasms. I am a man of substance, of flesh and bone, fiber and liquids—and I might even be said to possess a mind. I am invisible, understand, simply because people refuse to see me."

Rosenberg goes on to describe the lineup of shows planned for the fall season and to point his finger at those responsible for deciding to omit African American characters from their casts. "Whether through sins of commission or omission, television has spent decades being pretty much an equal opportunity offender." Rosenberg concludes:

> All these years later too many minority members "of substance, of flesh and bone, fiber and liquids," still remain invisible on too much of TV, characters who, like Ralph Ellison's here "might even be said to possess a mind." And based on these new fall shows, there's no cause for optimism.

Clearly it is possible to read Harold Rosenberg's essay without ever having read *Invisible Man.* But how much richer, how much more powerful his message becomes when coupled with the memory of Ellison's hero! It is the ability to tap that richness that I want my students to possess.

I would like to make a final comparison between contemporary literature anthologies and the 1901 Ginn edition for twelve-year-olds. Could many middle school students today negotiate the work of Hawthorne, Dickens, Tennyson, Elliot, Browning, or Thackeray with any degree of success? Even Robert Louis Stevenson, long considered the staple of any boy's reading life, is hard going for most students today. While I am not recommending the return to an exclusive diet of nineteenth-century authors, and while celebrating the growing body of young adult literature available to teenage readers, I urge that the literature chosen for classroom study be of the finest quality. If the chosen texts are difficult for young readers, then we must strive to make students better readers. Today, as in 1901, to open their eyes "to a clearer vision and nourish and inspire" their souls is an enormous task. I need the work of giants in hand to help me.

6

READING LITERATURE IN A STATE OF FLOW

*Stately, plump
Buck Mulligan
came from the
stairhead, bearing
a bowl of lather on
which a mirror and a
razor lay crossed.*

—James Joyce,
ULYSSES

Reading demanding literature need not be merely a grind. When students become caught up in the work of studying literature, the difficulties posed by the text seem manageable and the literature more accessible. One method for making this happen is to invite students to model writing of their own after the masters. When they are caught up in what Mihaly Csikszentmihalyi calls a "state of flow" and investing their own creativity into the reading process, the hard work of comprehension is doable.

In his collection of essays *A Voice from the Attic*, Robertson Davies describes the kind of readers I want my students to become: "those who read for pleasure, but not for idleness; who read for pastime but not to kill time; who love books, but do not live by books" (1990, 7). Davies defines a love of literature "not as a manifestation of fashion, not as a substitute for life, but as one of the greatest of the arts, existing for the delight of mankind." I measure my success in the classroom by the intellectual delight my students take in their reading. I want their hearts to leap up both when they behold a rainbow in the sky and when they read William Wordsworth's poem. I hope they find solace and surprise in the written word as students in my class and throughout their lives.

Arguably reading and writing about literature does little to prepare students for the real world. Critics see the study of even seminal works of literature as superfluous to helping students make a living. But making a living isn't enough. The young people entrusted to our care also need to extrapolate from reading literature how to make a life. And real life all too often poses moral dilemmas like the one Atticus Finch confronted in Harper Lee's *To Kill a Mockingbird* when he stood up for his beliefs in court and in so doing put his own children at risk. Walking a mile in Atticus' shoes, vicariously experiencing both his fear and his

**MY HEART
LEAPS UP WHEN
I BEHOLD**

My heart leaps up
    when I behold
A rainbow in the
    sky:
So was it when my
    life began,
So is it now I am a
    man,
So be it when I
    shall grow old
Or let me die!
The Child is father
    of the Man:
And I could wish
    my days to be
Bound each to
    each by natural
    piety.

*—William
Wordsworth*

courage, can help to prepare students for the hard choices they will make in their own lives. Students need to be prepared to make a living, to make a life, and—even in defeat, like Atticus Finch—to make a difference.

Students want to make a difference. One has only to witness wall after wall of urban graffiti to see how young people are driven to make their mark on the world. I always try to be on the lookout for ways students can express themselves that won't get them into trouble with the law. One method that has reliably engaged them in creative work is modeling. Walking in a writer's shoes can be a powerful way to learn about literature from the inside out. It also produces remarkable student poetry.

Modeling and Imitation

Some students are adept at counting beats and marking accents, but others find imitation a more effective method for understanding meter. If students are unsure how the iambic pentameter works, ask them to imitate a line of Shakespeare's, inserting words of their own in place of the bard's, following his rhythmic pattern. For example, students can take "The quality of mercy is not strain'd; / It droppeth as the gentle rain from heaven / Upon the place beneath" (*Merchant of Venice*, act 4, scene 1) and then use these lines to describe another virtue or vice. Paul came up with "The quality of hatred is not black; / It shineth as the brightest light from one / Who loathes another." Allison wrote, "The quality of ardor is not cold; / It burneth as the coals of hell / Inside a lover's heart." This is a wonderful vocabulary exercise as students search for synonyms that will work inside the line's metric structure. We printed out these Shakespeare-like lines with students' names attached and posted them on a bulletin board outside our classroom under the heading, Virtues and Vices. Students searched Google images for the virtues and vices they wrote about (with a little help from their teacher to make appropriate choices), printed them out, and illustrated the board with these as well. For a time, it significantly inhibited graffiti-production on that otherwise blank board.

Imitation or modeling also works for other aspects of form and style. I struggled for years trying to teach students about epic similes, extended comparisons that intensify the heroic stature of characters and events. I explain to students that Homer used similes to describe action in his story by comparing it with something his listeners would find familiar. I stumbled upon the idea of having students choose one of Homer's epic similes and adapt it to describe how they perform an ordinary act. I suggested they consider:

- how they eat a banana

- how they practice an instrument

- how they text a friend

- how they work out for soccer

- how they take a math test

Of course, students come up with better ideas than mine, but they often need examples to see just how wide a range of topics are acceptable. On occasion I have in my files an epic simile written by one of the students' older brother or sister. Reading these never fails to make kids smile.

Tenth-grader Joe Cafferky wrote, "As a hundred-year-old man stabs with withered fingers that bear the fork for a remaining pea on his plate, so did heavy-eyed, soccer-sore Joe pick at his hand-gathered corn flakes." Zara Qureshi crafted, "As a mouse scurries back to its hole, chased by a cat, and fearful for its life, so did Zara scramble about her messy room, gathering her papers for school." Modeling their own writing after Homer's, students developed an understanding of both the structure and the purpose of epic similes. They could see how Homer drew from something familiar (eagles swooping down for a kill) to describe what he imagined (Odysseus' gang routing out the suitors from his hall). Students now had some grasp of the technique and perhaps also the purpose of epic similes.

Some students are natural imitators. Once I saw how easily the epic similes were flowing, I asked students to use Homer's opening invocation to the muse as a model for the opening of an epic poem they might write someday about their odyssey through high school. For the moment we would be writing only the first page. I intended for this to be more than a creative writing exercise. I wanted students to play with language, but I also knew that many were struggling to make sense of their reading. I thought that appropriating Homer's lines for their own use would help students negotiate his language with greater ease. Geoff Adams, a tenth grader on the school's water polo team, penned the following parody of Albert Cook's 1967 translation of *The Odyssey*.

> **Tell me, Muse, about the too-much-to-do Geoff**
> **Who for many nights was sleepless with all work and no play**
> **In the pool he suffered many cramps in his legs,**
> **Striving for a life and his companions' company**
> **But he could not find his friends,**
> **For they were all out bowling.**

Along with having a bit of fun, these students were experimenting with seeing their own lives in a light-hearted heroic context. As Aiden Gray so eloquently describes in "Buried Life":

> But often, in the world's most crowded streets,
> But often, in the din of strife,
> There rises an unspeakable desire
> After the knowledge of our buried life;

EPIC SIMILE FROM HOMER'S *ODYSSEY*

"The attackers struck like eagles, crook-clawed, hook-beaked, swooping down from a mountain ridge to harry smaller birds that skim across the flatland cringing under the clouds but the eagles plunge in fury, rip their lives out—hopeless, never a chance of flight or rescue—and people love the sport—so the attackers routed suitors headlong down the hall, wheeling into the slaughter, slashing left and right and grisly screams broke from skulls cracked open—the whole floor awash with blood."

A thirst to spend our fire and restless force
In tracking out our true, original course;
A longing to inquire
Into the mystery of this heart which beats
So wild, so deep in us—to know
Whence our lives come and where they go.

Teenagers, although caught up in concerns about their appearance and who likes whom, worry deeply about their lives and where their lives will take them. When I offer students this invitation to describe something they experience every day in elevated language, they begin to see how they, like Odysseus, have embarked on a journey of self-discovery. Sonja Chen, a talented violinist in the school orchestra, wrote this invocation to the Muse:

Tell me, Muse, about the girl of many notes,
Who many hours practiced when she joined
Mr. Breen's Symphony Orchestra.
She saw many staff, and knew their notes;
With her violin she suffered many pains within her heart,
Striving for the day when she would be in tune.

I particularly liked the way students instinctively chose to write about an area of their lives in which they were struggling. The mock-serious tone they adopted seemed to allow the writers both to complain about their problems and at the same time to see them as archeypal obstacles that clutter every hero's path to glory.

In *The Hero with a Thousand Faces,* Joseph Campbell (1973) explains how the mythological hero ventures forth from the ordinary world into unexplored territory. There the hero meets unimagined obstacles, monsters with unthinkable powers, ogres who—on a bad day—may look much like the water polo coach or orchestra director. But the hero overcomes these obstacles, garnering a scar or two along the way, and ultimately triumphs, returning to the ordinary world with newly-found knowledge.

Few teenagers would immediately identify themselves as "heroes" or make the connection between their own messy lives and a hero's journey without some prompting. I show students Peter Stillman's (1985) definition of a hero to help broaden their perspective and trigger discussion.

To honor an individual with the exalted title of hero, we must be satisfied (although not always consciously so) that he has performed certain ritual-ized tasks and feats. Furthermore, his character must be essentially noble, although not unflawed. A hero must leave behind him, or overcome, the weaknesses and temptations we give in to, or his quest is doomed to failure. He must suffer privations, dangers and agonies beyond those we believe we're able to endure—even if he suffers them in connection with an apparently

HERO'S JOURNEY TALES FOR MIDDLE SCHOOL READERS

Dragonsong, Anne McCaffrey

A Wizard of Earthsea, Ursula LeGuin

Neverwhere, Neil Gaiman

Harry Potter and the Philosopher's Stone, J. K. Rowling

The Hobbit, J. R. R.Tolkein

Eregon, Christopher Paolini

The Golden Compass, Philip Pullman

Seaward, Susan Cooper

Redwall, Brian Jacques

Cupid, Julius Lester

The Talisman, Stephen King and Peter Straub

The Hitchhiker's Guide to the Galaxy, Douglas Adams

The Merchant of Death (Pendragon #1), D. J. MacHale

meaningless quest. Furthermore, he must act out his role alone. Although a hero figure may be surrounded by others, his is a spiritual solitude; as he moves deeper into the unknown, his solitude deepens too. (31–32)

We talk about heroes students have met in fairy tales, in literature, and in the movies who seem to meet Peter Stillman's guidelines. It is often important at this point to make the distinction between real-life heroes who run into burning buildings to save babies and archetypal heroes. I want students to think about how archetypal heroes point the way for the rest of us.

Kristin Thingstad's imitation of the beginning of Book II of *The Odyssey* situates her within this heroic context. Drawing from her experiences in marching band, Kristin demonstrates how she has suffered privations and agonies and ultmately triumphs.

> **And when the early-born, rosy-fingered dawn appeared,**
> **The dear daughter of Chester jumped from her bed**
> **Drew around her many layers of clothing for warmth,**
> **Slung the heavy tuba over her shoulder and**
> **The much-encrusted marching shoes beneath her aching feet,**
> **And went out onto the field, like a zombie to look at.**
> **At once Mr. Greene ordered the drum majors with their piercing voices**
> **To summon the musically-challenged band members to rehearse.**
> **The drum majors made summons, but the weary students moved slowly,**
> **Kristin set the brass tuba on her sloping shoulder.**
> **Not alone, but the lazy-footed marchers went along with her.**
> **If only Athene would have shed a divine grace about her now.**
> **Mr. Greene, a man bent from many marching seasons,**
> **Raised his baton, and then music was all we were.**

I was so impressed with what students had done that I created a display in the main office titled "Recently Discovered Fragments of Epic Poetry." It made a huge hit at Back to School Night. Parents loved seeing their children write like Homer.

Playing with Language

Alexis Angolano struggled whenever she had to write. So it came as a surprise to both of us when we discovered that she found epic poetry easier to generate than analytical prose. Reading her imitation of Homer, I saw how much I had underestimated Alexis' insight into what she read. Judging from the way she developed an argument, I assumed her understanding of the literature we had been reading was limited. However, looking at what she wrote here, I could see how deeply Alexis had internalized Homer's story. Comparing herself with Odysseus' struggling son Telemachus, Alexis reveals how clearly she understands the obstacles this young hero faces as well as those she herself faces daily:

> **And when the early-born, rosy-fingered dawn appeared,**
> **The body of Alexis rose without her soul,**
> **Took a quick shower, ate breakfast,**
> **And went out of her room like a harpy to look at.**
> **At once she ordered her parents to summon**
> **The light-haired siblings to breakfast.**
> **The parents made summons, and they quickly gathered together.**
> **And when they were gathered she went to the table**
> **Holding her hairbrush in her fist,**
> **Not alone but the sturdy barrettes came, too.**
> **Moreover Mrs. Jago had shed a divine grace around her.**
> **The family marveled as she sat down in her father's seat**
> **And the light-haired siblings gave way.**
> **The the designated carpool mom arrived**
> **A woman bent with age who knew numberless things**
> **She, too, had dear daughters who went with bright-eyed Alexis**
> **In the hollow minivan to South Burlington High, abounding in**
>   **teenagers.**
> **Jessica had been wounded by the savage principal in the hallowed halls.**
> **And another daughter Kelsie fell in with the drug crowd.**
> **Two daughters stayed always in their father's mansion**
> **But still she remembered the lost ones in grief and sorrow.**
> **For them she wept and then addressed the family:**
> **"Listen to me now, family, in what I say.**
> **We have not once met for much too long**
> **And now who has called us together: And to which of the young women**
> **Or of those who are older, has there come so great a need?"**

When I talked with Alexis about what she wrote, she said that this piece just seemed to come to her, that the words just "kinda flowed." I thought of Mihaly Csikszentmihalyi's (1990) theory of flow and began to see a possible explanation for Alexis' newly tapped source of expressive power. Csikszentmihalyi posits that a person can become so involved in work or in a project that nothing else seems to matter. He calls this the theory of optimal experience. When caught up in a state of flow, a person finds the work itself so enjoyable that distractions and even time disappear. Intensely involved, the person will often continue to work even at great cost, simply for the sheer pleasure of doing it. Czikszentmihalyi explains:

> Contrary to what we usually believe, the best moments in our lives are not the passive, receptive, relaxing times—although such experiences can also be enjoyable, if we have worked hard to attain them. The best moments usually occur when a person's body or mind is stretched to its limits in a voluntary effort to acommplish something difficult and worthwhile. (3)

Imagine if we could transform schoolwork into a series of flow-producing activities. Imagine moving students from a position of resistance to reading difficult books to Csikszentmihalyi's state of optimal experience. Reading *The Odyssey* may not be what most kids think of when urging one another to "go with the flow," but they might be surprised to discover how pleasurable time spent with Homer can be.

Alexis continued to produce her best work when assignments invited her to make connections between her own life and her schoolwork. For a project in which students were asked to create a metaphor for education using a small, empty box as a starting point, Alexis created a ceramic brain and mounted it atop the box. She called her piece "Thinking Outside the Box." Over time, Alexis' analytical writing began to reflect an integration of her creative and intellectual sides. Toward the very end of the year she had the sobering experience of being suspended from school. Looking back at the Homeric imitation that she had written in October, I wondered if Alexis had had an intimation of what an odyssey her tenth-grade year would turn out to be.

Another feature of epic poetry that students often find odd—and, as a result, creates a stumbling block to their reading—is Homer's use of epithets. Epithets are short, stock words or phrases that define a distinctive quality of a person or thing. They are often reoccurring, as in the "wine-dark sea," "many-wiled Odysseus," and "cloud-gathering Zeus." Their purpose is twofold. Epithets provide a quick thumbnail sketch of a character or object. The repetition allowed the original singers a moment to recall what comes next.

For homework during our first few days reading *The Odyssey*, I asked students to list all the epithets they could find as they read. When they retured to class, students read to the class from their lists. In Book II they found: bronze-covered heaven, grain-giving earth, bright-eyed goddess Athene, aegis-bearing

Zeus, and two-handled cup. I quickly realized that they didn't recognize epithets that took the form of an appositive, as in "Nestor, breaker of horses" or "Nestor, the Gerenian horseman."

Once students had the sound of an epithet in their heads, I invited them to create a few of their own. I asked them—offering assurance that what happens in English class stays in English class—to write an epithet for their least favorite teacher, their mother or father, their best friend, their pet, a movie star, a figure in the news, the President. Students enjoy the exercise so much that they almost forget they are studying poetry. While they are in this state of flow, we return to reading the text. Along with teaching students about epithets from the inside out, I was also sending students the message that Homer didn't compose as he did simply to make life more difficult for readers. While this is an unexamined belief in most teenagers' minds, it is nonetheless a powerful one. I want students to see how Homer played with language for the sheer pleasure he took in words. He was probably in what Mihaly Czikszentmihalyi would call a state of flow.

TESTING THAT TEACHES

*E*very time a teacher of literature gives an objective test, students' confidence in themselves as readers is undermined. The very act of posing questions whose answers will be judged as correct or incorrect sends wrong messages to students: that there is only one right answer, that their teacher is the source of all correct information, and that the purpose of reading is to answer questions posed by someone else. Unless these messages are the ones we want students to receive, we should abandon such tests forever.

My primary instructional goal is to create a community of readers and writers peopled with students who both can and do read and write. Therefore, it does not make sense for me to ask students to match "Penelope" with the description "Odysseus' long-suffering and faithful wife." If any students do not know the accuracy of this description after we have spent almost four weeks reading the epic, I would hope that I already know this from my assessment of the students' class participation (or lack thereof). Why punish those students by putting them through the ordeal of an objective test—and possibly facilitating cheating—when I should already have more than enough information culled from formative observations to assign a grade? Why waste valuable class time this way? If you doubt that this is true, the next time you give an objective test, jot down how you think each student will do before you correct their tests. I'll wager there are few surprises.

The Limits and Uses of Objective Tests

Objective tests also foster a competitive spirit in the classroom. Test results encourage students to label one another as smarter-than-me or dumber-than-me, attitudes that are a detriment to classroom discussion. Consider it from a student's point of view. It's hard to feel good about contributing emerging ideas to a conversation on Monday when you have just been handed a paper emblazoned

It was the best of times, it was the worst of times, it was the age of wisdom, it was the age of foolishness, it was the epoch of belief, it was the epoch of incredulity, it was the season of Light, it was the season of Darkness, it was the spring of hope, it was the winter of despair.

—Charles Dickens,
TALE OF TWO CITIES

with a flaming red D from Friday's quiz. Teachers contradict themselves when, in one breath, they tell students to say what they think about a piece of literature, and in the next, ask them to fill in the name of Victor Frankenstein's father on an objective test. Often even the most astute readers will find they can't remember this level of detail on demand. Nor is it always important for students to be able to. Does making grade-percentage distinctions between readers who can recall plot details encourage students to read more deeply and more thoughtfully? I think not. Does it make our grades more accurate? Hardly.

Just as when students write about literature they need to feel confident enough to use their own ideas in their essays, when students read, they need to have the confidence to explain their interpretations to others. Ideally, every voice will have weight and substance and will add to the group's collective understanding of the text. For this to happen, students must respect one another's varied interpretations and regard one another as thinkers. There can be no "dummies" in this community. The operation of the pecking order among teenagers is a horrible thing to witness. It causes students both to silence themselves and to close their ears to anyone who looks or thinks differently from them. Teachers are relatively powerless to influence this behavior outside the classroom. Inside the classroom, however, we can either reinforce the status quo or establish a different kind of order, one where powerful ideas rule.

I had a unfortunate situation in class a few years ago. One student could not open his mouth without four other boys jeering. Matt, a bright and thoughtful

QUESTIONS NOT TO ASK ABOUT SHERMAN ALEXIE'S
THE ABSOLUTELY TRUE DIARY OF A PART-TIME INDIAN:

1. Who told Junior he should leave the reservation?
   a. His grandmother
   b. Rowdy
   c. His sister
   d. His teacher

2. The Rearden basketball team beat the reservation team in their first game.
   a. True
   b. False

3. When did Junior say his dad loved him the best he could?
   a. When he left the reservation
   b. On Father's day
   c. On the first day of school
   d. On Christmas

tenth-grade student, had trouble expressing himself and tended when he spoke to circle around his point for several minutes before stating it. But Matt also often saw things in the literature that everyone else had missed. I came down hard on the boys for their rudeness, but was not satisfied that even when they stopped, they were doing anything more than obeying me. What I wanted was for them to see how much they needed Matt's thinking as a complement to their own. Then I came up with the idea to put these four young men and Matt in a group and pose them a difficult literary problem to solve. Their task was to explain to the class how Paul in Erich Maria Remarque's *All Quiet on the Western Front* was deeply ambivalent about his role as a soldier when he returned to his town from the battlefield. Without Matt, these boys were in danger of looking like fools. Suddenly they hung on his every word, asking him questions, listening to and copying out his somewhat tedious answers. Their presentation, with someone other than Matt as spokesperson, was excellent.

Apart from the educational drawbacks of using objective tests to measure literary understanding, good multiple-choice questions, the kind that appear on Advanced Placement Literature and Language exams, are extraordinarily difficult to write. It is a poor use of your professional time to labor over the creation of the perfect distracters and stems that don't cue the correct response. Teachers too often use quizzes to play "gotcha" with students who they think, or know, aren't doing the reading. Instead of writing, copying, and correcting quizzes, spend those minutes talking with the students you fear are falling behind to find out why.

Today's grade books are computerized and visible to students, parents, counselors, and administration. As a result, many principals now expect teachers to enter a grade per week for every student. While this might make sense in mathematics, it works against language arts instruction if the mandate fosters an increased use of quizzes or forces teachers to assign points to reading notes taken on Lois Lowry's *The Giver*. How I get around the dictum is to enter weekly participation grades. I include many different kinds of performances—contributing to discussions, working collaboratively in groups, bringing books to class, completing homework reading—under the broad category of "participation." While some might consider my observations to be highly subjective, I would argue that such measures assess students' literacy development more authentically than quiz-like instruments.

I have found a use for the ubiquitous multiple-choice exams found in online study guides, though. It is sometimes important after investing weeks of instructional time with a long book to have students review key character names, places, and events before asking them to write about it. I locate and make copies of a multiple-choice test on the book, put students in groups, and ask them to answer as many questions as they can. After ten minutes I tell them they can use their books. After twenty more minutes I tell them they can seek help from another group. Five minutes before the bell rings I post the correct answers on the board and tell students that only tests with 100 percent correct responses will be accepted. The result? Every student has reviewed details from the book. Every student gets an A. And I didn't have to make up a single question.

Objective Tests Are Not College Prep

Some argue that objective testing prepares students for college, yet the students who go on to do well at the university level are those who read widely with understanding, who speak articulately about what they have learned, and write with confidence. Objective tests don't develop any of these qualities in learners.

Questions are the key to understanding literature. Students must have space to ask real questions, ones they genuinely want answered. Demanding their quick response to objective test questions discourages such thinking about literature. Besides, the issues we choose to emphasize—for example, the differences between Brutus' and Cassius' rhetorical styles—may not be what interested a student when reading *Julius Caesar*. A student may be more interested in the political power struggle between Antony and Octavius; therefore, this is what that reader remembered most about the play. A teacher constructing an objective test would be, in effect, punishing the Antony/Octavius reading while rewarding those whose reading matched the teacher's Brutus/Cassius reading. It is obvious how unfair this approach is, regardless of whether you can justify it by saying, "But we talked about the funeral orations at length in class." Our job as literature teachers should be to model reading and thinking about a text, not to dictate meaning. Because objective tests deny students their right to a defensible interpretation, they actually discourage both reading and thinking.

Objective tests do a grievous disservice to anyone trying to foster a love of reading and literature. Take a moment to think about the last good book you read. What stayed with you? It is probably neither the characters' names nor the name of the city where the story took place. What most likely stayed with you is a feeling for the book, a message the author conveyed, a sense of the fictional world you inhabited as you read. How would you feel about taking a test on this book where you were asked true-or-false questions about character motivation?

I know such a test would severely undermine the pleasure I took from the last book I read, José Saramago's *Blindness*. When I finished the novel, I could not with any certainty tell you the main characters' names. Does this make me a poor reader? Should I be punished for remembering the haunting narrative voice and the hellish world the characters descended into rather than plot details? Though I am itching to talk with someone about the book, it is to compare my response with another reader's. I'm not rushing to the Internet to see what literary scholars have written. I'm more interested in the views of other amateur readers whose views may deepen my understanding of José Saramago's rich and perplexing tale. For someone—anyone, even the author—to be set up as

"To say that you have taught when students haven't learned is to say you have sold when no one has bought. But how can you know that students have learned without spending hours correcting tests and papers? . . . Check students understanding while you are teaching so you don't move on with unlearned material that can accumulate like a snowball and eventually engulf the student in confusion and despair."

— *Madeline Hunter*

arbiter of what a book means contradicts everything we know about reading literature. Why would I practice in my classroom that which I do not believe is true for myself as a reader?

The challenge to those of us who object to right-and-wrong-answer tests of literary understanding is to devise ways of assessing students' reading that actually teach them more about what they have read. I want to use assessment to deepen student learning. To this end I asked a class of tenth graders who had just finished reading *The Odyssey* to write about a major character in the epic most like them. They were to explain the similarity using examples from their own life as well as from the text. Here is Susan Madden's response.

> **Zeus-born, son of Laertes, Odysseus of many devices resembles me the most out of all the characters in *The Odyssey*. I can relate to him because in the whole epic his purpose is to see his family and someday reach sunny Ithaca. Like Odysseus, I am often sad because I know what it is like for one's family to be so far away, mine being in Mexico. I don't have to go through**

the dangerous adventures Odysseus experiences, but I do have to wait a long time before seeing them again.

When in the land of the Phaeacians, a singer comes to town and relates the story of the battle at Troy, Odysseus' own story. Odysseus shed a tear, trying to hide it from the hospitable Phaeacians. A couple of weeks ago I saw a television show about Puebla, Mexico, what I call my land. It showed the town's churches and schools and the town square. These things are part of my story and my life. It made me sad to be so far away, and I cried. Odysseus and I grieve when each hears his own story.

Reading Susan's response left no doubt in my mind that she had (1) read the book and (2) understood what she read. As well as achieving these primary assessment goals, the prompt offered students the opportunity for further learning by inviting them to see the heroic dimensions of their own lives. This does not happen when students match character names with quotations. Class results on the "test" did not fall in a bell-shaped curve because many more students were able to be successful here than a grade distribution chart would predict. Does this mean their teacher has abandoned rigor in her instruction? Not to my way of thinking. Susan Madden's analysis of Odysseus demonstrates recall of details, reading comprehension, and insight into character motivation. The fact that such achievement was possible for most of the class should be cause for celebration. Student success should be our goal, not a cause for worry about grade inflation.

In one unsuccessful paper, a boy compared himself with Achilles solely on the basis of their shared strength and bravery. While applauding his strong self-image, I was critical of the absence of evidence from Achilles' visit with Odysseus in the underworld. It seemed to me that this student was simply tapping what he already knew about the Greek hero Achilles rather than citing examples from *The Odyssey* to support his claim. This kind of assessment instrument can separate those who have read a text with care from those who have not.

As I read the set of essays I was able to discern the extent to which students had developed a relationship with Homer's epic poem. For some it was a passing acquaintance. For others it was a bond. This is the kind of information I need to help me determine the appropriateness of the text as well as the quality of my instruction. Had I differentiated instruction enough to allow all students access to this demanding work? Had I provided multiple ways for students to demonstrate their emerging understanding throughout the course of the unit? The purpose of formative assessment is to provide teachers with the feedback they need to adapt instruction to students' needs. It is a process to assess students' "formation" as readers. Multiple-choice exams don't give me this kind of information. Reflective student writing does.

Unconventional Summative Assessment

One spring when my seniors had finished reading *Crime and Punishment,* I was at a bit of a loss as to how to assess their reading. We had had such powerful discussions about the book that I didn't need to check for understanding. They already had a paper on their outside reading book due on Friday, so I was reluctant to assign another essay. I fumbled around for a while, and then had one of my best ideas in ages. Since it would require introducing a seemingly unrelated piece of literature, I begged my students to indulge me. I promised that the lesson would ultimately make sense.

I handed out copies of Wallace Stevens' poem "Thirteen Ways of Looking at a Blackbird." We read the poem together and then I asked students to choose their favorite stanza and write about it for five minutes. I had them turn to a partner and read their stanza and explain their thoughts before we talked about the poem together. As always, students were puzzled but enchanted by Stevens' language and imagery. For homework I invited students to write a poem, modeled on Stevens' poem, titled "Thirteen Ways of Looking at Raskolnikov."

The next day I asked if anyone would like to read what he or she had written, hoping a brave few would volunteer. Almost every hand went up. What followed was an extraordinary display of these students' personal and private interpretations of Dostoevsky's novel. I wish I could include every one of them here. If you haven't read Wallace Stevens' poem in a long time, treat yourself to a rereading before you peruse these students' poems.

Grace Chang is the youngest of three sisters. The first two were both valedictorians at Santa Monica High School. When she wrote this poem Grace was going through a very difficult time because her B in Calculus meant that she would not be able to follow in her sisters' footsteps. Grace's home language is Chinese.

With middle school students I like to use Pablo Neruda's *Odes to Common Things* and Gary Soto's *Neighborhood Odes* as models for this assessment. I ask students to choose an important object from the book we have studied and to write an ode in praise of it. You will be amazed at the way students instinctively explore the significance of the object in terms of the work as a whole.

THIRTEEN WAYS OF LOOKING AT RASKOLNIKOV
by Grace Chang

1
Among twenty snowy mountains
The only moving things
Were the eyes of Raskolnikov

2
He was of three minds
Like an axe
On which there was
The smear of three people's blood.

3
The guilt is nothing
The suffering is everything

4
A man and two women
Are three.
A man and two women and an axe
Are one.

5
He does not know which is more revolting
The repugnance of the blood
And gore spilt by his hands
Or the memory of them

6
A red shadow on the floor
Has an undecipherable cause

7
O thin men of Petersburg
Why do you imagine murderous painters?
Do you not see how Raskolnikov
Walks among you?

8
He knows noble accents
And lucid, inescapable rhythms;
But he knows, too,
That the painter is not involved
In what he knows.

9
When Raskolnikov fled the scene,
It marked the beginning
Of the suffering he would endure

10
At the sound of Raskolnikov's sighs
Even the pawnbroker's customers
Would cry out sharply

11
He rode over Connecticut
In a glass coach.

Once, a fear pierced him,
In that he thought
What on earth was he doing
In Connecticut, so far away from Russia

12
Sonia is crying
Raskolnikov must be lying

13
It was evening all afternoon
It was sunny
And it was about to be sunny
Raskolnikov sat
In the cedar-limbs of Porfiry's chair

Though Nadia Popienko had lived in Russia until she was nine and continues to speak Russian at home, her access to Dostoevsky was through English. Needless to say, her parents were vey pleased that she was reading this novel that had been so much a part of their education in Moscow.

THIRTEEN WAYS OF LOOKING AT RASKOLNIKOV
by Nadia Popienko

1
Among twenty bustling taverns
The only moving thing
Was the mind of Raskolnikov.

2
I was of three minds
Like one in delirium
Like Raskolnikov.

3
Raskolnikov in the summer heat
Is only a small part of God's work

4
Crime and punishment
Are one.
Crime and punishment and redemption
Are one.

5
I do not know which to prefer
Being extraordinary

Or being ordinary
The ability to kill
Or the ability to love

6
He swung the axe.
The blood gushed
As from an overturned glass.
The mood traced in the shadow
An undecipherable cause.

7
O thin men of St. Petersburg
Why do you dream about Lazarus?
Why do you not see how hopelessness
Entangles the feet
Of the children about you?

8
I know noble accents
And lucid, inescapable rhythms;
And I know, too,
That I am capable
Of experiencing Raskolnikov's fate.

9
When Raskolnikov left society
He could feel free in prison.

10
At the sight of Raskolnikov
Roaming in the darkness
Even strangers cry out
"Murderer! Murderer!"

11
He rode over to Siberia
With an unquiet mind.
Once, a fear pierced him
In that he mistook
His own shadow
For Napoleon.

12
Life continues.
Raskolnikov must find redemption.

13
It was night all nine years
It was dark
And it was going to be dark
Until it was allowed
For there to be light.

Najla Chaudhry is a quiet, serious, intense student. She said little during our class discussion of *Crime and Punishment* (with thirty-eight students in the class, it was often difficult to get a word in), but her body language made me feel that she was thoroughly engaged in our work with the novel. When I read her poem, I knew for sure.

THIRTEEN WAYS OF LOOKING AT RASKOLNIKOV
by Najla Chaudhry

1
On the dark, sinister staircase
The only moving things
Were the legs of Napoleon.

2
He was of three minds
Literally.

3
The door rattled in the silence
It was a small part of the punishment.

4
A man and two women
Are one.
A murderer and a prostitute
And an axe and a Bible
Are one.

5
I do not know which to detest more,
A drunken axe-murderer
Or a drunken scholar.

6
There is no window
And if there were there would be no glass.
The shadow of a man
Crosses in and out, to and fro.

The couch
Traces the outline of his body
Where he spends half his day.

7
Oh extraordinary Russian mouse
Do you not see how the cat
Purrs with pouncing games on his mind?

8
I know noble accents
And lucid, inescapable rhythms;
But I know, too,
That one's lips taste like dirt
After kissing the ground.

9
When blood is shed
It leaves its mark
On a pair of dirty socks.

10
At the moment
When dark turns to light
The truth will astound,
And confuse.

11
He sent himself to Siberia
On a half-dying mule.
Once, a fear nagged him
And he mistook
The shadow of his equipage
For a beautiful stallion.

12
The women are dead.
Someone must have killed them.

13
It was evening all the way through.
It was snowing
There was no snow on the ground.
The convict sat in his cell.
Free.

While Grace, Nadia, and Najla's poems demonstrate their own gifts for language—for all three in their second language!—every student in the class generated a thoughtful poem. Some borrowed heavily from Wallace Stevens' lines. Others were technically inept. But whatever their merit as poetry, these responses demonstrated a deep and powerful response to *Crime and Punishment*. That night I scribbled over my lesson plans, "Among thirty-eight senior students / The only thing not moving / Was their awestruck, lucky teacher."

The Essay as Experiment

The most common way that I assess student learning is through essays. I believe students should work in the style of Michel de Montaigne. Disillusioned with sixteenth-century discourse, Montaigne experimented with a new form of personal writing. He knew that what he was creating fit no traditional category so he simply called his work *essais,* meaning attempts, or trials, or experiments. I want my students' essays to be experiments in thinking.

In his introduction to *The Norton Book of Personal Essays,* Joseph Epstein (1997) describes his own approach to essay writing as a form of discovery:

> I sometimes make notes recalling anecdotes, facts, oddities of one kind or another that I wish to include in an essay, but where precisely in the essay they will be used I cannot say in advance. As for a previous design or ultimate goal for my essays, before I write them I have neither. The personal essay is, in my experience, a form of discovery. What one discovers in writing such essays is where one stands on complex issues, problems, questions, subjects. In writing the essay, one tests one's feelings, instincts, thoughts in the crucible of composition. (15)

I love that phrase, "the crucible of composition." Clearly student writers need more guidance and structure than an accomplished essayist like Joseph Epstein, but I fear that when we insist on conformity to artificial structures like the five-paragraph essay, they will never know the intellectual joy of discovering what they think as they write. I am not suggesting that we allow students to turn in whatever random thoughts come to them as they compose on their keyboards. Good writing is carefully crafted. But the best writing is always inspired.

Of all types of writing, writing about literature may seem the least practical. Who, apart from scholars and English majors, analyzes poetry after the age of eighteen? Even book reviewers don't write the kinds of essays commonly assigned in school. Why do teachers devote so much effort to developing an arcane skill? Because writing about literature disciplines the mind. It challenges students to look closely into what they read and express clearly and powerfully what they find there. Writing about literature invites students to construct personal interpretations and then support their interpretations with evidence from the text. Such writing requires students to pause and think hard about what they have read. While some teachers (and many students) feel that having to write an essay about a book diminishes the pleasure they take in reading, I think otherwise. Knowing that they will be writing an analytical essay about what they are reading often lends urgency and intensity to our classroom conversations. Writing becomes a vehicle for exploring students' understanding of what they have read. If the product, a 700–1,000-word essay on Karen Hesse's *Out of the Dust,* seems artificially school-based, so be it. The intellectual process that students have employed to compose the paper is genuine.

I require students to write about literature because writing helps develop literary understanding. Composing an analytical essay forces students to reread with a purpose and to scrutinize the text, as well as to analyze the author's craft. It also demands that they do this work for themselves. No matter how hard I try to engage all my students in classroom discussions, I have never been able to ensure that everyone takes part. Writing demands individual performance. As a result, each student essay provides me with a window through which to view the particular student's emerging competence as a reader and writer. I have ceased to be surprised when I discover a stunningly insightful essay from a student who hardly murmured a word in class. Many individuals can achieve on paper what they find difficult to demonstrate aloud in class.

Students write poorly about literature when they don't understand what they are writing about. All too frequently the teacher develops a series of lessons for guiding students through a demanding piece of literature. Once the final page of the book has been turned, the teacher assigns a paper, usually focusing on an aspect of the text that has been thoroughly presented and discussed. Why are we surprised when all the essays sound alike? Though I sometimes ask students to write to a prompt, students seem to write more authentically when the idea for the essay is their own. Requiring them to develop their own focus for a paper also places responsibility for content squarely on the writer. This freedom has greatly diminished complaints such as "I hated the prompt" or "I didn't understand the question." My students seem to take more care with their essays when writing about something that intrigues them than when writing about a question that intrigues me. They have more reason for revision when the ideas being showcased are not borrowed but are their own. Analytical responses to literature that emerge from their own interpretations of a work—even when imperfectly accomplished—always seem to have more heart.

Unfortunately, some teachers cling to objective tests and rigid forms of the essay for the power these structures allow them to wield over students. But this is not real power, and students know it. Real power resides in the literature. I teach to help students have access to this power for themselves.

READING THE MEDIA

The Common Core Reading Standards in Literature are explicit about the importance of teaching students to analyze audio, video, or live interpretations of the literature they read. Anchor Standard 7 states that students should be able to "integrate and evaluate content presented in diverse media and formats, including visually and quantitatively, as well as in words." As teachers think about how to implement this standard, it will be important to keep the focus on analysis. We need to design lessons that invite students to take a critical stance toward the media they consume.

The Kaiser Family Foundation study (2010) mentioned in the Introduction is the third in a series of national surveys of teenagers' consumption of entertainment media. Drew Altman, Ph.D., president and CEO of the foundation, reports that "the amount of time young people spend with media has grown to where it's even more than a full-time work week. When children are spending this much time doing anything, we need to understand how it's affecting them—for good and bad." The study doesn't interpret the data pejoratively, leaving it to parents and educators to determine the significance of their findings.

> For the first time over the course of the study, the amount of time spent watching regularly-scheduled TV declined from 2004–2009 by 25 minutes a day. But the many new ways to watch TV—on the Internet, cell phones, and iPods—actually led to an *increase* in total TV consumption from 3:51 to 4:29 hours per day, including 24 minutes of online viewing, 16 minutes on iPods and other MP3 players, and 15 minutes on cell phones. All told, 59% (2:39 hours) of young people's TV-viewing consists of live TV on a TV set, and 41% (1:50 hours) is time-shifted, DVDs, online, or mobile.

"The bottom line is that all these advances in media technologies are making it even easier for young people to spend more and more time with media," said Victoria Rideout, Foundation Vice President and director of the study. "It's more important than ever that researchers, policymakers and parents stay on top of the impact it's having on their lives." (2010)

The ubiquity and influence of media in students' lives makes it ever more important to help teenagers be critical consumers of what they see and hear. Children are bombarded with seductive visual images. Every time they gaze at television, a computer, or a movie screen, they need to exercise judgment. Moreover 34 percent of children aged eight to eighteen say they have rules in their home about how much television they can watch or online games they can play. Interestingly, those with any rules typically consume three fewer hours per day than students with no rules. The question for English teachers is what kinds of rules we should set for ourselves regarding the use of media within the language arts curriculum. We need to find a balance that incorporates both the Common Core Standards and the media into our literature lessons.

Common Core Standard 7 for Reading Literature

Grade 6
Compare and contrast the experience of reading a story, drama, or poem to listening to or viewing an audio, video, or live version of the text, including contrasting what they "see" and "hear" when reading the text to what they perceive when they listen or watch.

Grade 7
Compare and contrast a written story, drama, or poem to its audio, filmed, staged, or multimedia version, analyzing the effects of techniques unique to each medium (e.g., lighting, sound, color, or camera focus and angles in a film).

Grade 8
Analyze the extent to which a filmed or live production of a story or drama stays faithful to or departs from the text or script, evaluating the choices made by the director or actors.

Grades 9–10
Analyze the representation of a subject or a key scene in two different artistic mediums, including what is emphasized or absent in each treatment (e.g., Auden's "Musée des Beaux Arts" and Breughel's *Landscape with the Fall of Icarus*).

"Education is the point at which we decide whether we love the world enough to assume responsibility for it and by the same token to save it from that ruin, which, except for renewal, except for the coming of the new and the young, would be inevitable. An education, too, is where we decide whether we love our children enough not to expel them from our world and leave them to their own devices, nor to strike from their hands their choice of undertaking something new, something unforeseen by us, but to prepare them in advance for the task of renewing a common world."

—*Hannah Arendt*, Teaching as Leading

Grades 11–12

Analyze multiple interpretations of a story, drama, or poem (e.g., recorded or live production of a play or recorded novel or poetry), evaluating how each version interprets the source text. (Include at least one play by Shakespeare and one play by an American dramatist.)

(*Common Core State Standards*, 2010)

I celebrate the Common Core Standards' recognition of the importance of learning to read the media and to make critical comparisons across artistic mediums. Today's media-savvy teenagers are often surprisingly naïve in their consumption. I am hopeful policy makers will recognize that in order to do the deep analytical work described in Standard 7, teachers and students will need easy access to technology and the Internet.

The Uses and Abuses of Film in the Classroom

Every moment of class time is precious. By the time a teacher has taken attendance, made a few announcements, turned on the video, turned down the lights, and hit *PLAY*, there are often only about forty minutes of a class period left for the movie. This means that the typical feature film will take three class periods to show. If a teacher shows five movies over the course of the school year—which given the number of film adaptations of classic novels available and the reluctance of students to read makes the temptation to do so very great—students will have spent fifteen days or three weeks of class time viewing. In a school year of 180 days, this means students will have spent 8 percent of their instructional time in

English class watching movies. What worries me most about this use of time is that often when the lights go down and the screen lights up, teenagers hit their internal relax button and shut down their critical faculties. A few put their heads down for a snooze. Unless the lesson has been skillfully framed, most students consider a period watching a movie as a period off.

Teachers unintentionally foster this attitude by scheduling films for days when they themselves must be absent. The number of substitute lesson plans that read "Show film" is legion. Substitute teachers don't mind because it doesn't take much effort to press the *PLAY* button. Kids don't mind because they feel they aren't being asked to do any work. What isn't clear is how much learning is going on. For students already consuming seven and a half hours of media every day, the hour spent watching a movie in class is just one more.

In order to increase the learning, viewing needs to go hand in hand with analysis. Let's take a look at the grade 8 standard that asks students to "analyze the extent to which a filmed or live production of a story or drama stays faithful to or departs from the text or script, evaluating the choices made by the director or actors." Students who have read *A Christmas Carol* find much to discuss as they watch Jim Carrey's interpretation of Ebenezer Scrooge in the 2009 Disney animated rendition of the book. Rather than showing the film in its entirety as a "treat" for having finished reading the story, choose selected scenes where the film version stays faithful to or reinterprets the text. After each scene from the film, ask students to jot down their views, talk about them with a partner, and discuss their insights with the whole class. Postpone evaluation ("I like the movie better." "No, I hated it.") for as long as you can. Taking sides often shuts down conversation. Learning takes place as students develop their argument regarding the extent to which the film remained faithful to Dickens' story and themes. As they garner evidence from the book and movie to support their claim, their thinking about both deepens.

I also like showing the same scene from a Shakespeare play in several iterations. We view the "To be or not to be" speech as delivered by Sir Laurence Olivier, Mel Gibson, and Ethan Hawke and then discuss how the various interpretations reflect the time the film was made and the expectations of audiences. While I have the films in hand, I also like to show students the various portrayals of Ophelia by Jean Simmons, Kate Winslet, and Julia Stiles. While showing these, I display for students paintings of Ophelia by John Millais, John William Waterhouse, Anton August Hebert, and others that I have found online. In this manner we "analyze the representation of a subject or a key scene in two different artistic mediums." We compare these visual images with the filmmakers' decisions regarding casting, costume, and makeup as well as with our initial mental images of Ophelia based on our reading of the play.

Teachers need to be on guard against inadvertently structuring students' viewing of a film in such a way that it discourages students from reading the text.

For example, the 1946 film version of *Great Expectations* is considered a classic. Viewing this movie, therefore, would seem the ideal solution for slow or reluctant readers who, if they could be persuaded to persevere, might well need six weeks to complete Dickens' (1994) four-hundred-page novel. But as powerful as the graveyard scene is, these students would be much poorer for never having visualized the following scene from the book for themselves.

> "Hold your noise!" cried a terrible voice, as a man started up from among the graves at the side of the church porch. "Keep still, you little devil, or I'll cut your throat!"
>
> A fearful man, all in coarse grey, with a great iron on his leg. A man with no hat, and with broken shoes, and with an old rag tied round his head. A man who had been soaked in water, and smothered in mud, and lamed by stones, and cut by flints, and stung by nettles, and torn by briars; who limped and shivered, and glared and growled; and whose teeth chattered in his head as he seized me by the chin.
>
> "O! Don't cut my throat, sir," I pleaded in terror. "Pray don't do it, sir."
>
> "Tell us your name!" said the man. "Quick!"
>
> "Pip, sir." (1–2)

This is powerful prose, rich in detail and full of passion. To offer students a film version in place of Dickens' sentences seems a poor substitute. Teenagers will take the substitute, of course. But though they will come away with the outline of the story, they won't have learned how to read nineteenth-century literature. Most will tell you they don't care, but how could they care when they have no idea what they are missing? High-quality film adaptations of novels and plays clearly have a place in the language arts curriculum—after students read the novel.

Another way to integrate critical viewing into the curriculum without eating into class time is to have students watch films on their own time. In a variation of literature circles, I ask groups of students to choose a book to read and a film to view together. In the pairings I have looked for films that do not faithfully recreate what the writer has done but rather that provide interesting adaptations of the original story.

- *Emma* by Jane Austen and the film *Clueless*
- *One Flew Over the Cuckoo's Nest* by Ken Kesey and the film
- *The Color Purple* by Alice Walker and the film
- *Do Androids Dream of Electric Sheep* by Philip K. Dick and the film *Blade Runner*
- *The Joy Luck Club* by Amy Tan and the film

- *The Strange Case of Dr. Jekyll and Mr. Hyde* by Robert Louis Stevenson and the film *Mary Reilly*

- *Breakfast at Tiffany's* by Truman Capote and the film

- *The Talented Mr. Ripley* by Patricia Highsmith and the film

- *The Age of Innocence* by Edith Wharton and the film

- *Never Let Me Go* by Kazuo Ishiguro and the film

- *Holes* by Louis Sachar and the 2003 film

- *The Secret Garden* by Frances Hodgson Burnett and the 1993 film

- *Alice in Wonderland* by Lewis Carroll and the 2010 film

- *The Miracle Worker* by William Gibson and the 1963 movie with Anne Bancroft

- *The Chronicles of Narnia* by C. S. Lewis and the 2005 film

- *The Diary of a Wimpy Kid* by Jeff Kinney and the 2010 film

- *Swiss Family Robinson* by Johann D. Wyss and the 1960 film

- *The Princess Bride: S. Morgenstern's Classic Tale of True Love and High Adventure* by William Golden and the 1987 film

The particular point of interest in *The Color Purple* and *The Joy Luck Club* pairing is that in each case the authors were heavily involved with the making of the films. I invite students to research this aspect of the film's interpretation of the original text. One caveat I have regarding these novels is that the Internet offers hundreds of essays for sale about both *The Color Purple* and *The Joy Luck Club*. Rather than discouraging me from exposing students to these fine works of contemporary literature, I use the occasion of this viewing assignment to talk about intellectual integrity. While I refer to our school policy on the various punishments for representing another's work as their own, I am more interested in helping students see how they short-change themselves when they plagiarize.

You will want to be sure to obtain signed parent permission for students to view any R-rated films. Be sure to include a wide range of films for students and their parents to choose from. It can also be a good idea to show your list to your department chair and/or principal before sending it home. Administrators hate surprises.

Almost every classic has been considered at one time or another for production by a filmmaker. This is for good reason. Classic stories have—among other things—unforgettable characters, a riveting plot line, and an enduring message. It is a recipe for success on the big screen as well as on the small page (or e-reader). Once students have read the novel and seen the movie, I ask students to write a comparison/contrast essay about the two experiences. A by-product of this writing assignment is that students find it quite natural to help one another develop ideas for their papers. Often less able readers see things in the film that their peers have missed. More able writers help these students organize what they have seen into coherent form. Viewing the film together outside school time seems to help build community in the classroom.

The goal of this assignment is to help students think about how filmmakers reinterpret and re-imagine original texts and to consider how true to the original a particular interpretation has been. In order to accomplish this task, students must hone their viewing skills along with their reading skills. There is no need to beat students over the head with learning the standards when every classroom task is aligned to them.

Fine Art in the Language Arts Curriculum

Before suitable technology was available, my use of fine art was limited by the number of museum posters I could afford to purchase or by the handful provided as overhead transparencies by textbook publishers. The Internet and LCD projectors have changed all that. Now I have the museums of the world at my fingertips. Fine art can be a powerful vehicle for teaching summarization, interpretation, point of view, analysis, and close reading. Many students who have difficulty interpreting W. H. Auden's "Musée des Beaux Arts" can, if they know the myth of Icarus, insightfully analyze Pieter Bruegel's *Landscape with the Fall of Icarus*. We practice "reading" the visual text image by image, color by color, line by line, exploring the artist's use of atmosphere and tone, and then apply these same methods of analysis to a literary text. Once we have analyzed Auden's poem, I ask them to read William Carlos Williams' poem "Landscape with the Fall of Icarus." An added benefit to this work is that students are being exposed to a body of fine art as they learn to interpret poetry.

When in search of a pregnant pairing, I don't look for an illustration of the literary text but rather a representation in another media of a similar theme in visual form. I want to help students see how the same themes can be expressed in poetry, art, music, dance, and drama. I also want them to explore the extent to which the medium influences the artist's message. The following pairings of fine art and literature have triggered rich conversations in my classroom:

- *Pool Parlor* by Jacob Lawrence and the poem "We Real Cool" by Gwendolyn Brooks

- *Pearblossom Highway* photo collage by David Hockney and the poem "The Road Not Taken" by Robert Frost

**HOW TO READ
A PAINTING**

- Choose three words that describe the feeling in this painting.

- What do you think is happening in this scene?

- What part of the picture was your eye drawn to first?

- How did the colors in the painting make you feel?

- What about the lines and curves?

- If this were a scene from a story, what kind of story would it be?

- What do you think is the most important object in this picture?

- Paintings by Jean Michel Basquiat and the poem "Life Doesn't Frighten Me" by Maya Angelou

- Andy Warhol's Marilyn Monroe and Mao paintings and "Famous" by Naomi Shihab Nye

Another variation on pairings across media is to have students analyze a painting and then read poems that were inspired by the canvas. Often lines in the poem cause students to see aspects of the painting they had overlooked.

- *Starry Night* by Vincent Van Gogh and the poem "The Starry Night" by Anne Sexton

- *The Disquieting Muses* by Giorgio di Chirico and "The Disquieting Muses" by Sylvia Plath

- *Girl Before a Mirror* by Pablo Picasso and the poem "Before a Mirror" by John Updike

- *House by the Railroad* by Edward Hopper and the poem "Edward Hopper and the House by the Railroad" by Edward Hirsch

- Photographs of the Vietnam Memorial in Washington, D.C. and the poem "Facing It" by Yusef Komunyakaa and "The Vietnam Wall" by Alberto Rios

- *Nude Descending a Staircase* by Marcel Duchamp and the poem "Nude Descending a Staircase" by X. J. Kennedy

A creative sequel to this lesson is to send students to the Internet to find a painting they find compelling—it pleases me a great deal when students look for another painting by an artist we have discussed—and then ask them to write a poem of their own with the same title, inspired by what they see in the visual image. Meeting Common Core Reading Standards can be a pleasurable as well as a rigorous endeavor.

MOTIVATING
RELUCTANT READERS

T he Common Core Standards alone will neither turn students into
readers nor improve student achievement. It is going to require the
concerted effort not only of teachers but of our whole society—a society that sometimes seems aggressively anti-intellectual—in order for America
to become a nation of readers. Many teenagers are outspoken in their distain
for learning, at least for the kind of learning they are currently being offered
in school. Working with these students, many of whom can read but refuse
to read, is the greatest challenge middle and high school teachers face. I find
inspiration in the words of Matthew Arnold. Along with being the author of
the much-anthologized, melancholy poem, "Dover Beach," Matthew Arnold
was an educational reformist who urged the English to compare their school
system with those in other countries. He believed that a radical rethinking of
teaching practices was needed, and that the place to start was with self-criticism.
In the preface to *Culture and Anarchy*, Arnold (1932) explains that his purpose
for writing the book was:

> to recommend culture as the great help out of our present difficulties;
> culture being a pursuit of our total perfection by means of getting to know,
> on all the matters which most concern us, the best which has been thought
> and said in the world; and through this knowledge, turning a stream of
> fresh and free thought upon our stock notions and habits. (6)

I have tried in the preceding chapters to offer ways for making demanding and rich literature accessible to teenage readers. Like Arnold, I feel we are
in some "present difficulties," and that we have to some extent brought them
upon ourselves. For too many students, literature has been short-changed in the

If I had been some years younger, what with shame, weariness, and disappointment, I believe I had burst into tears. As it was, I could find no words, neither black nor white, but handed him the letter, and sat down to the porridge with as little appetite for meat as ever a young man had.

— Robert Louis
Stevenson,
KIDNAPPED

curriculum. They no longer are taught "the best of which has been thought and said in the world." Teachers, and especially English teachers, may be students' principal access to these works. Literature is not the only place where young people can learn about the best of what has been though, but it is one place.

In middle schools all over the nation the 1990s brought with them a significant shift in focus toward the promotion of self-esteem over curricular rigor. I watched this happen firsthand in my district. When I taught at Lincoln Junior High School we expected students—not always with success—to read demanding literature and to study history. When my son attended the same school, then Lincoln Middle School, from 1994–1998, language arts and social studies were combined into a double period with the same teacher, sometimes an English teacher and sometimes a social studies teacher. The academic rigor in both disciplines suffered. Instead of being assigned demanding texts to read and write about, students made "Who Am I?" mobiles and constructed dioramas of historical events. While the intentions behind such a movement to promote students' self-esteem were pure, the unintended consequence was that more, not fewer, students arrived at the high school without the machinery to read demanding texts. It was not uncommon for many first-semester ninth graders to have three Ds or Fs on their report cards at the first grading period. Highly motivated students from the more affluent side of town continued to do well, partly because their parents had never stopped feeding them books and taking them to museums, but the very students the self-esteem movement was designed to serve foundered.

Research conducted between 1991 and 2004 by the Consortium for Chicago School Research found that the most significant predictor of a student dropping out was how that student performed in ninth grade. As Elaine Allensworth, a researcher for the consortium, dug deeper into the data she found that the most common reason students earned Ds and Fs on their first report card in high school was attendance. Students are smart. As they realize they are bound to fail, they stop coming to school to preserve their self-esteem. Why show up if you can't do the work? Once students begin this downward spiral, their chances of graduating decrease dramatically. The consortium has worked tirelessly with Chicago public schools to reverse this trend through intensive, individual counseling and curricular reform in grades 6 through 8 (Chicago public schools are organized K–8 and 9–12). Instead of making the curriculum easier for students, schools need to engage students in academic work that matters to them, projects that involve their own inquiry into the issues that surround them, and texts that challenge them to think.

The Common Core Standards have sought to address the lack of rigor in many middle school language arts programs. They require seventh graders to "compare and contrast a fictional portrayal of a time, place, or character and a historical account of the same period as a means of understanding how authors of fiction use or alter history" and eighth graders to "analyze how a modern work of fiction draws on themes, patterns of events, or character types from myths, traditional stories, or religious works . . . including describing how the material is rendered new." Mobiles and dioramas will be of little assistance in preparing students to meet these standards. Neither will worksheets or skill-and-drill lessons. Instead, we need to employ creative instructional methods for engaging students in their reading. Ask any coach. Genuine self-esteem is built on success and vice versa.

Modeling Instruction After What Good Readers Do Naturally

In order both to help students comprehend demanding literature and to meet Common Core Standards, I begin with the behaviors of good readers. According to research by Michael Pressley and Peter Afflerback (1995), excellent readers are extremely strategic readers. Often without realizing that they are doing it, strong readers:

- overview a text before reading

- determine what is most important in what they are reading

- use prior knowledge to make sense of new learning

- predict what is likely to come next in a text

- construct an interpretation of a text as they read

- draw inferences from what they read

- determine the meaning of words they don't understand, especially when the word seems critical to making sense of the text

- use techniques such as underlining, rereading, note-taking, visualizing, summarizing, paraphrasing, and questioning strategically to focus their reading

- engage in an imaginary conversation with the author

- anticipate or plan for the use of knowledge gained from the reading

Although many remedial reading programs have turned these behaviors into reading strategies, each with its own catchy acronym, I don't think this is the best method for helping reluctant readers develop the habit of doing these things naturally. Too often the strategies insert a layer of artificiality onto the act of reading. Do you keep a reading log? When was the last time you filled in a wish-bone/fishbone graphic organizer to explain relationships between characters? This is not to say that such tools can't be helpful for making what is transparent for good readers visible to all students. But too many students think their work is done once they complete the graphic organizer. It's the thinking that these tools represent, the habits of mind, that we want students to acquire. Teachers need to be strategic in their use of classroom time so that students spend a brief amount of time practicing strategies and the bulk of their time reading.

There is support from cognitive science for this approach to instruction by strategy. In his column for the *American Educator,* "The Usefulness of *Brief* Instruction in Reading Comprehension Strategies," Daniel Willingham explains that more than 500 studies over the past twenty-five years demonstrate that teaching students to monitor their comprehension, use graphic organizers, summarize, answer and generate questions, work collaboratively, and recognize story structures improves reading comprehension. But he goes on to say that:

> Based on my reading of the research and my understanding of cognitive science, I think that the answer may be that successfully implementing a reading comprehension strategy is not a skill at all. It may be more like a trick in that it's easy to learn and use, and the only difficulty is to remember to apply it consistently. . . . Teaching reading strategies is a good way to give developing readers a boost, but it should be a small part of a teacher's job. Students can learn them quickly and they are effective, but they appear to deliver a one-time boost. Acquiring a broad vocabulary and a rich base of background knowledge will yield more substantial and longer-term benefits. This knowledge must be the product of years of systematic instruction as well as constant exposure to high quality books, films and conversations. (2006–2007, 45)

One approach for ensuring that students receive both years of systematic instruction and constant exposure to high-quality books is to carve out time in the school day for a reading seminar. The Olathe School District in Olathe, Kansas, has implemented a semester-long class that every sixth through eighth grader on grade level or above in reading is required to take along with their English language arts class. The stated vision for the program is, "We want [each student] to be ravenous for reading. We want him to pick up a book and set out on a journey, feed an interest, explore a passion. . . . We want [each student] to become not just a school reader but a lifetime reader who understands that reading is a free pass to entertainment, adventure, and a rich, productive life" (Zimmerman and Hutchins 2003).

In a class modeled along the lines of a reader/writer workshop, students engage in authentic practices: reading for pleasure, talking about what they read, sharing good books, and reflecting on their own progress as readers. The class also provides conference time for teachers to offer help to individual students with special reading needs. The program is structured to provide purposeful and appropriately rigorous reading experiences geared to students' needs and interests. To support this goal, the district is working to make every classroom a literacy-rich environment teaming with books.

Though teachers have a great deal of instructional flexibility, the period is organized around an agreed-upon framework:

Middle School Reading Seminar

Beginning of the Hour

- Book Talk(s)/Reading Minute/Read-aloud

- "Gathering"

- Close Reading/Modeling/Minilesson

Middle of the Hour (Independent reading or literature circles)

Students:

- Read

- Write

- Discuss

Teachers:

- Observe/listen/record

- Offer differentiated instruction

- Hold individual conferences

- Reads

End of the Hour

- Reader's Chair

- Closure/Reflection

Testimonials from teachers, students, and parents indicate that many middle school students are enjoying reading for the first time and actually choosing to read in their free time. Several students called Reading Seminar their favorite class and were acutely disappointed to learn they had to change classes the next semester. The program has the potential to help all students learn to be the kind of strategic readers Pressley and Afflerback describe. It also avoids the common pitfalls of overteaching books students are able to read on their own and thus destroying a good book with our harping on symbolism and irony, or under-teaching and simply assigning books that students need our help with. In the spirit of full disclosure, Mary Jo Fox, language arts and Title 1 coordinator for the Olathe School District, is my sister, and Kay Haas, the Olathe Instructional Projects Specialist, a colleague from the NCTE Executive Board. The most telling Reading Seminar testimonial for me came from a sixth grader who remarked, "I never knew I liked reading so much!"

Pairing Young Adult Books with Classic Texts

To those who say that contemporary teens can't relate to the characters in classical literature, I would suggest rereading Chapter VI of *Great Expectations*. The convict Magwitch has just confessed to the "crime" Pip committed by stealing food and drink from Pip's sister's house. Though Pip is relieved not to have been caught, he is also troubled by this first experience of his own duplicity.

> My state of mind regarding the pilfering from which I had been so unexpectedly exonerated, did not impel me to frank disclosure; but I hope it had some dregs of good at the bottom of it. I do not recall that I felt any tenderness of conscience in reference to Mrs. Joe, when the fear of being found out was lifted off me. But I loved Joe—perhaps for no better reason in those early days than because the dear fellow let me love him—and, as to him, my inner self was not so easily composed. It was much upon my mind (particularly when I first saw him looking about for his file) that I ought to tell Joe the whole truth. Yet I did not, and for the reason that I mistrusted that if I did, he would think me worse than I was. (37)

What teenager, which of us, has not known such a moment? Most of us want to be good and tell the truth as we have been taught to do, but then circumstances complicate matters. Decisions in real life, or in good literature, seldom appear in black or white. As we learn with Pip how to negotiate this gray area of compromised morality, we experience a fall from grace. Some call this growing up. Much of the skill in bringing demanding literature to life for students is a matter of helping them see themselves in Pip and other protagonists.

In *The Gutenberg Elegies, The Fate of Reading in an Electronic Age,* Sven Birkerts (1994) writes about how "adolescence is the idea laboratory for the study of reading and self-formation" (89).

> How does reading work on the psyche during what is surely its most volatile period of change? There is no pinning it down, naturally, but we might begin with the most obvious sort of answer: the role of specific books and characters. We get reports of this influence all the time in interviews and memoirs. The subject tells of living with Tom Sawyer or David Copperfield or Elizabeth Bennet. There follows the desire to do what Tom did, to be like young Elizabeth. These recognitions are eventually externalized as ideas and in that form guide the behavior along after the

spell of the reading passes. I vividly remember situations in which I acted in a certain way—more bravely, more recklessly—because I believed that that was what Jack London would have done. (89–90)

One method of helping students begin the process of identification is to start with characters a bit more like them than Pip. I always have students reading two books at the same time. One, like *Great Expectations*, that they need instructional help with, and another young adult novel that with a little help from their friends in a literature circle they can read on their own. I choose books for the literature circles that have main characters that experience similar feelings and difficulties as the characters in the novel we are studying together. In this manner students begin to see that though the clothes may be different, the inner yearnings are the same.

Let's use some of the literary characters Sven Birkerts mentions and some of my own favorite characters as examples of the kind of reading curriculum I am recommending. All of the young adult titles I have listed for literature circles are Newbery Medal or Honor books. Young adult titles often go out of print quickly. Using Newbery winners both helps ensure that the books will continue to be available and will assist you in garnering approval for their use.

Core Text

Tom Sawyer, Mark Twain

Literature Circle Titles

The Mostly True Adventures of Homer P. Figg, Rodman Philbrick

Elijah of Buxton, Christopher Paul Curtis

A Year Down Yonder or *A Long Way from Chicago,* Richard Peck

Hoot, Carl Hiaasen

Surviving the Applewhites, Stephanie S. Tolan

****

Core Text

Little Women, Louisa May Alcott

Literature Circle Titles

When You Reach Me, Rebecca Stead

The Evolution of Calpurnia Tate, Jacqueline Kelly

Feathers, Jacqueline Woodson

Getting Near to Baby, Audry Couloumbis

Our Only May Amelia, Jennifer L. Holm

****

Core Text

Call of the Wild, Jack London

Literature Circle Titles

Crispin: The Cross of Lead, Avi

Hattie Big Sky, Kirby Larson

A Girl Named Disaster, Nancy Farmer

What Jamie Saw, Caroline Coman

The Midwife's Apprentice, Karen Cushman

Rather than scheduling periodic literature circle meetings over the course of their reading of a novel, I bring students together only after they have finished the whole book. This more authentically replicates adult book clubs. It also helps to avoid the chaos caused when some students have read only a few chapters while others have finished the novel. I have students use a Venn diagram to compare the main character in their literature circle book with the main character in the core work we are studying together. Filling in the graphic organizer helps to focus their discussion on the issue of characterization. Another assignment students enjoy is writing a dialogue between, for example, Tom Sawyer and Homer P. Figg. In order to create these imaginary conversations, students must think beyond the text, extrapolating what characters like Tom and Homer might have to say to one another and in so doing what these characters have to say to them.

I am not ashamed of my desire to shape my students' behavior, in Mathew Arnold's words, to turn "a stream of fresh and free thought" upon their "stock notions and habits." I believe there are ways of conducting oneself that are preferable to others. I try to offer students some of "the best which has been thought and said in the world," in the hopes that they will engage in the important work of making this world a better place.

Constructing Lessons That Provide Additional Support

It sometimes seems that an invisible barrier exists between the book and the student. Too many of my students can read but won't. And the longer they persist in this refusal, the more their reading skills deteriorate from lack of use. Like a leg in a cast, their reading muscles atrophy. I don't need standardized test scores to identify such students. After just a few days in class they identify themselves. Signs to look for include a reluctance to carry any book at all around school (I may have just handed out copies, and already the student asked if he can store it in the classroom), a shrug of the shoulders when we go around the class describing what we read over the summer, or a desire to sit at a desk as far away from me as possible.

In *Why Don't Students Like School: A Cognitive Scientist Answers Questions About How the Mind Works and What It Means for the Classroom*, Daniel Willingham posits that much of the work we ask students to do is either too easy or too hard. When a text is too easy, students are quickly bored. When it's too hard, students toss the book aside and refuse to try. Classroom texts and tasks that require mental effort need to be challenging enough to engage students yet not so difficult that they give up in frustration. Willingham asserts that "people are naturally curious, but we are not naturally good thinkers; unless the cognitive conditions are right, we will avoid thinking" (2010, 3).

When I have a class of students determined to avoid thinking, I try to design lessons that engage students' curiosity without daunting them overmuch. As we begin work on a demanding novel, one of the most important things to establish is a strong sense of the main character. After we have read or listened to an audio version of the first chapter, I sketch an outline of a head on the board and ask students for words that describe the main character. I fill the open mind with students' contributions and add a few of my own. (Students stay on task better if you have them copy what you are compiling down for themselves.) I then ask students to reread the first chapter looking for evidence to support one or more of the character traits we identified. The rereading serves two purposes.: (1) It provides an opportunity for those who haven't yet read the opening pages to catch up without fuss; and (2) it sends students back to what are probably the most carefully crafted pages in the whole book. So many clues to the meaning of a work are embedded in the introduction, yet we often read these pages quickly with minimal understanding.

I then go through the character traits we have charted inside the open mind and call on students to contribute the examples they have found in the text that support this generalization about the main character. Placing a sticky note on each student's desk, I ask students to choose one of the traits we have identified and as they read tonight's assigned pages to place the note where they find another example of this trait. We begin class the next day by going around the room having each student state the character trait he or she chose, read the selected passage, and explain how this quotation demonstrates the trait. The exercise helps lend purpose to students' homework reading without unduly interrupting their reading. It is really helpful for developing the kind of commentary I want to see when they go to write about this character. Best of all, this pedagogically sound lesson doesn't generate a single piece of paper for me to read.

A Literary Education Is Priceless

Once while playing chauffeur to a station wagon full of fifteen-year-old boys, friends of my son, James, I eavesdropped on their conversation about compulsory military service. After several minutes of debating whether girls should be drafted, the subject shifted to war. They had all recently read *All Quiet on the Western Front*.

Pat: Look at what happened to Paul. His teacher and everybody in the town had him all hyped up about being a soldier and then Bam! He's in the middle of hell.

Kevin: Paul had no idea what he was getting himself into when he signed up. They fed him a bunch of lies about honor and glory and the Fatherland. If there was a war and I got drafted, I wouldn't go.

James: Not even if your mom said you should?

Kevin: Mothers don't know anything. Paul's mom still didn't get it even when Paul came back on leave all messed up in his head. She thought he looked good in his uniform.

Pat: I don't believe you, Kevin. You're Jewish. You wouldn't have fought Hitler?

Kevin: OK, I'd fight Hitler but that's different.

James: I think it's always different. And I think guys like Paul always get screwed in war. It was a good book, though, Mom. Thanks for the ride.

As the boys piled out of the car, they had no idea how happy they had just made me. *All Quiet on the Western Front*, a book they had read at my behest, caused them to turn a stream of fresh and free thought onto their own stock ideas about military service and war. These teenagers weren't showing off their literary education but rather using it to explain what they meant.

When I was nine an aunt who knew I loved to read gave me a box of books. The children's hospital where she worked was discarding Annie Fellows Johnston's The Little Colonel series, and she hated to see them dumped in the garbage. The books were written at the end of the nineteenth century and set in what remained of plantation life following the Civil War. The main character is a headstrong little girl nicknamed the Little Colonel after her Confederate hero grandfather. I adored reading about this little girl's exploits and outbursts. I reveled in her boldness. The Little Colonel, brash and outspoken, embodied everything I, whiny and bookish, was not.

Unfortunately volume three of the twelve-volume set, *The Little Colonel's House Party,* was missing. I devoured the eleven I owned and for years imagined the wonderful things that must have happened at that party. I knew the missing volume must be the best book in the world. Many years later my husband found this book in an antiques market in central Ohio—the book I had been waiting for thirty-five years to read. I brought the worn copy to class. Students were open-mouthed when I told them he had paid $68 for this tired-looking copy, but they could see my eyes shining in anticipation of turning its pages. What I discovered as I read was more curious than any children's house party. Politically incorrect in any number of ways, the book stands as a charming period piece. Characters behave decently toward one another. The Little Colonel may be willful and spoiled, but she is genuinely contrite when her haughtiness hurts others or when she learns how self-absorption has blinded her to those less fortunate than herself. These are issues that I have had to struggle with in my own character all my life. How strange that I should have somehow recognized even as a child that this would be the case. The Little Colonel (even before I new how the word *colonel* was pronounced) provided me with a remarkable model for behavior. Self-improvement is the last thing on the mind of a child, yet for avid readers, it always seems that the books we need find us.

Another thing that interested me about Annie Fellows Johnston's series was the complexity of its vocabulary and sentence structure. Writing for young children's amusement, Johnston employed sentences like these:

> Under the blossoms rode the Little Colonel, all in white herself this May morning, except the little Napoleon hat of black velvet, set jauntily over her short light hair. Into the cockade she had stuck a spray of locust blossoms, and as she rode slowly along she fastened a bunch of them behind each ear of her pony, whose coat was as soft and black as the velvet of her hat. (1921, 13)

I imagine this sentence would rate quite highly in terms of its readability level or Lexile score, yet Annie Fellows Johnston's books were wildly popular among young readers in the 1920s and 1930s. I doubt that children were smarter then. I do think we underestimate the kinds of sentences young readers can understand when the story is a compelling one. Here is another passage to compare against the prose textbooks find appropriate for fourth- or fifth-grade readers:

> The dust flew, dogs barked, and chickens ran squawking across the road out of the way. Heads were thrust out of the windows as the two vanished up the dusty pike, and an old graybeard loafing in front of the corner grocery gave an amused chuckle. A little while later the three white envelopes were jogging sociably along, side by side in a mailbag, on their way to Louisville. But their course did not lie together long. In the city post-office they separated, and sent on their different ways, like three white carrier-pigeons, to bid the guests make ready for the Little Colonel's house party. (24)

Johnston used complex syntax and employed a level of vocabulary that would challenge many of my ninth graders. On a single page I found: *imperious, imposing,* and *picturesque.* The text also incorporates dialect without recourse to footnotes.

> "Oh, deah," croaked the Little Colonel like a dismal raven, as she waited at the head of the stairs for the girls to finish dressing. "This is the last mawnin' we'll all go racin' down to breakfast togethah! I'm glad that Betty isn't goin' away for a while longah. If you all had to leave a the same time, it would be so lonesome that I couldn't stand it." (248)

A child who grows up reading children's literature that invites him or her to hear language as spoken by characters who speak very differently from him or her will have little difficulty in high school with the dialect in *Great Expectations, Huckleberry Finn, Their Eyes Were Watching God,* or *The Color Purple.* Sandra Stotsky contends in *Losing Our Language* (1999) that in response to demands for wider representation and easier-to-read texts in elementary textbooks, publishers have eliminated much of the literature that once prepared students for the challenging academic and literary texts they will be expected to read in high school and college. Marilyn Adams develops this argument in an article titled "Advancing Our Students' Language and Literacy: The Challenge of Complex Texts" (2010–2011), suggesting that "failing to provide instruction or experience with 'grown up' text levels seems a risky course toward preparing students for the reading demands of college and life" (5). Adams believes that making readings easier for students denies them the very language, information, and modes of thought they need most in order to develop intellectually. The literature we offer children, and particularly the literature we teach in school, should be both culturally diverse and stylistically complex. These are not mutually exclusive.

Sandra Stotsky's argument brings us to the issue of classical versus multicultural literature (we had to get to it sometime). Mark Twain or Toni Morrison? William Shakespeare or Athol Fugard? Ernest Hemingway or Leslie Marmon Silko? Rather than argue over which titles to remove from the curriculum in order to make room for new works, have students read twice as many books. It is easier said than done, but this is by far the best solution.

It isn't that today's teenagers aren't reading, but much of what they read is relatively lightweight. Compared with classical literature, the prose style of most of what students read online is comparatively simple. While there is nothing inherently simplistic about online writing, the environment favors short sentences and easy-to-read prose styles. In *The Shallows: What the Internet Is Doing to Our Brains* (2010), Nicholas Carr, author of the widely circulated *Atlantic* essay, "Is Google Making Us Stupid?" laments the effect the Internet is having on us. If we who have already developed the reading habit find ourselves spending more and more time twittering away, imagine how difficult it is for

THEMATICALLY PAIRED TRADITIONAL AND CONTEMPORARY CLASSICS

- *The Diary of a Young Girl* by Anne Frank with *The Book Thief* by Markus Zusak

- *A Tree Grows in Brooklyn* by Betty Smith with *Angela's Ashes* by Frank McCourt

- *Romeo and Juliet* by William Shakespeare with *Like Water for Chocolate* by Laura Esquivel

- *Jane Eyre* by Charlotte Brontë with *Annie John* by Jamaica Kincaid

- *The Red Pony* by John Steinbeck with *All the Pretty Horses* by Cormac McCarthy

- *Lord of the Flies* by William Golding with *John Dollar* by Marianne Wiggins

- *The Red Badge of Courage* by Stephen Crane with *The Things They Carried* by Tim O'Brien

- *Fathers and Sons* by Ivan Turgenev with *Dreaming in Cuban* by Cristina Garcia

- *Brave New World* by Aldous Huxley with *Never Let Me Go* by Kazuo Ishiguro

- *The Fall* by Albert Camus and *The Reluctant Fundamentalist* by Moshin Hamid

- *The Odyssey* by Homer with *The Road* by Cormac McCarthy

young readers who aren't wholly convinced of the value of books to make time to read let alone to read difficult books. Observing his own changing reading habits, Carr wonders if the time he spends on the Internet has diminished his capacity for concentration and contemplation. If we want our students to have the stamina to read literature, we will need to help them increase their capacity to concentrate and contemplate.

Coda

One of the oddest things about being a teacher is that you can sometimes find yourself a character in the stories students tell. I know that the day Christina fainted in my arms has passed into Santa Monica High School Folklore. The class was talking about John Gardner's novel *Grendel,* and someone was using a particularly gruesome passage as evidence for a point he was making. As the monster began to tear the queen apart, Christina, pale and wan, walked to the front of the room. She whispered into my ear, "Mrs. Jago, can I please go to the . . ." at which point she collapsed. Lifting her head from the carpet I turned to the class and remarked, "Ah, the power of literature."

How this story has been told and retold over the years, I shudder to think. My guess is that the part where I call the school nurse and Christina is diagnosed with a bad case of missing breakfast is somehow omitted. Students tell the story to make a point. Mrs. Jago is crazy about literature.

Constructing and Using Lists

However authoritative a book list pretends to be, most are actually quite arbitrary. Lists include and exclude texts based upon criteria that are sometimes transparent even to the list makers. When the Modern Library released its list of the hundred best novels written in English in the twentieth century, it was met with outrage. How could James Dickey's *Deliverance* be better than anything Joseph Conrad ever wrote? How is it possible that not a single book by Doris Lessing, Nadine Gordimer, Patrick White, Toni Morrison, or John Updike appears? Is *Ulysses* really the best book written in the twentieth century?

"So make your own list," said the publishers of the Modern Library list, and they proceeded to provide a website where readers could create alternative lists. I like that response. Readers enjoy making lists of "best" books almost as much as they like poking holes in other people's lists. I know I am always keen to see the *New York Times* "10 Best Books" at the end of any calendar year if only to quibble with their selections or to gloat where my own list corresponds with theirs. James Strickland (1997), English professor at Slippery Rock University, Pennsylvania, offers his take on the nature of book lists:

> Nick Hornby's characters in *High Fidelity* are constantly playing a game that involves picking the top five something: top five sub-titled films: *Betty Blue, Subway, Tie Me Up! Tie Me Down!, The Vanishing, Diva* . . . top five favorite recording artists, top five side one track ones (mine: Janie Jones, the Class from *The Clash* . . .). The reason that his characters can play that game, and we can by extension, is that the items on the list are debatable. If there were agreement about the all-time top five Dylan songs, there'd be no point making a list. The fun is in offering a different set of selections.

If each of us made a list of the top five works to read in 10th grade, there would be some agreement, but each of the items would probably be worthy of inclusion. The inclusively compromising among us might suggest combining the lists to make a top twenty-five works for 10th grade. But what of the 26th book? And the 27th? Any mathematician will tell you there is no last number—there's always one more to add (n+1). (17)

The lists that follow make no claim to authority. They are the personal choices of one reader: me. I got the idea from a monograph by Anna Quindlen (1998), *How Reading Changed My Life*. In it, she describes her own life as a child reader. She explains how the habits she acquired endured. Her extended essay is a testimonial to reading.

> By the time I became an adult, I realized that while my satisfaction in the sheer act of reading had not abated in the least, the world was often as hostile, or at least as blind, to the joy as had been my girlfriends banging on our screen door, begging me to put down the book—"that stupid book," they usually called it, no matter what book it happened to be. While we pay lip service to the virtues of reading, the truth is that there is still in our culture something that suspects those who read too much, whatever reading too much means, of being lazy, aimless dreamers, people who need to grow up and come outside where real life is. (9)

Dedicated readers often face such unspoken criticism, and it may be part of the reason many of my tenth-grade students, particularly boys, are so reluctant to be seen with a book in their hands. Most students do not look up to the readers in the midst. Readers are considered nerds or strivers. A few popular kids may be secret readers, but like the secret writers, they mostly keep their passion for books to themselves. Within teenage culture, being a reader carries little status.

For that reason, I don't waste my breath trying to persuade reluctant readers that books are "cool." Instead I try to find the one particular book that just might hook one particular reader. For Maria, a fifteen-year-old who boasted that she had never finished a book in her life, it was a paperback biography of Tejana singer Selena. For tough-talking Chris, it was Paul Beatty's *White Boy Shuffle*. In class I draw comparisons between these stories and their contemporary heroes with the heroes in the stories we are studying. How was Selena's conviction about her talent similar to Beowulf's conviction regarding his own strength? How were the troubles Gunnar faced in *White Boy Shuffle* a bit like Odysseus'? Can you see any similarities between how Gunnar dealt with drugs and how Odysseus behaved in the Land of the Lotus Eaters? Working with students like Maria and Chris over the course of a school year, I can increasingly influence their reading habits. I shared with their class this passage from Anna Quindlen's first chapter:

In books I have traveled, not only to other worlds, but into my own. I learned who I was and who I wanted to be, what I might aspire to, and what I might dare to dream about my world and myself. More powerfully and persuasively than from the "shalt nots" of the Ten Commandments, I learned the difference between good and evil, right and wrong. One of my favorite childhood books, *A Wrinkle in Time*, described that evil, that wrong, existing in a different dimension from our own. But I felt that I, too, existed much of the time in a different dimension from everyone else I knew. There was waking, and there was sleeping. And then there were books, a kind of parallel universe in which anything might happen and frequently did, a universe in which I might be a newcomer but was never really a stranger. (6)

I asked students first to write about and then to talk about what they thought of Quindlen's observations. Had a book ever made them feel like this?

José: I kinda felt like that when I read *Always Running*. Roberto said it was good so I looked at it and, yeah, it made me think about my neighborhood and how Luís almost really messed up his life with dope. I guess it gave me some ideas about good and bad.

Roberto: Everybody knows drugs mess you up. What I liked about that story was the way Luís shows how even though you know they are bad news, most kids still use them. I'm always gonna remember that scene where he's sitting in the dried up L.A. River Basin and almost dies.

Me: Why?

Roberto: Luís has this like out-of-body experience like he's already dead but then he comes back. It's scary.

Me: What about books you have read that were set in places that are nothing like L.A. or people that you'll ever meet?

Michelle: You mean like Wealthow in *Beowulf*? What a stupid name. I keep thinking how she should never have married that old king. I mean she has this great hair, and I know she was saving her people and all that but I would never have done it. He's too old. Those scenes in their bedroom gave me the creeps. (Diana is conflating plot details from John Gardner's *Grendel* with details from *Beowulf*, but I didn't want to interrupt.)

José: She was a babe.

Me: Anna Quindlen talks about learning about good and evil from books. Did any of the stories we read make you feel this way?

Michelle: Not really. Well, maybe the way when Grendel told his side of the story you start to see how people we call monsters might have another side. I mean, maybe there's a reason some of the bangers out there are doing what they do. Maybe nobody ever cared about them the way nobody but his weird mother ever cared about Grendel.

It seemed to me that at least within the classroom, these students no longer found it a nerdy thing to be talking about books. The next challenge was to help them learn how to find their way to books on their own. Anna Quindlen's whimsical lists of book titles gave me an idea. Hers included *Ten Mystery Novels I'd Most Like to Find in a Summer Rental, 10 Books I Would Save in a Fire (If I Could Save Only 10),* and my very favorite, *10 Books That Will Help a Teenager Feel More Human.* I wondered if I could come up with short lists that students might find as intriguing as I found Quindlen's. I offer these lists to see your own thinking. They were enormous fun to compile. At your next English Department meeting, why not pass around headings of your own devising—*10 Books for Teachers on the Verge of a Nervous Breakdown, 10 Books for English Teachers Who Have Considered Quitting When the Rainbow Is Not Enuf* (with apologies to Ntozake Shange)—and see what titles emerge? And don't forget to invite students to make up their own lists for summer reading—*10 Books for Guys Who Play GTA (Grand Theft Auto), 10 Books to Make You Cry.* It's a great way to encourage kids to declare themselves as readers and talk about books.

10 Short Classics for Readers Short on Time

I Heard the Owl Call My Name, Margaret Craven

The Prince and the Pauper, Mark Twain

Winesburg, Ohio, Sherwood Anderson

Lady Susan, Jane Austen

The Stranger, Albert Camus

Hard Times, Charles Dickens

The Ballad of the Sad Café, Carson McCullers

One Day in the Life of Ivan Denisovich, Alexander Solzhenitsyn

Metamorphosis, Franz Kafka

Animal Farm, George Orwell

10 Books for Girls Certain They Will Never Meet Prince Charming

Franny and Zooey, J. D. Salinger

Stop Pretending: What Happened When My Big Sister Went Crazy, Sonya Sones

The Help, Kathryn Stockett

Doctor Zhivago, Boris Pasternak

Bonjour Tristesse, Francoise Sagan

Mr. and Mrs. Bo Jo Jones, Ann Head

The Character of Rain, Amélie Nothomb

Theft, Peter Carey

After Dark, Haruki Murakami

The Other Boleyn Girl, Philippa Gregory

10 Books for Boys (and Girls) Who Love Action and Hate Long Descriptions of Drawing Rooms and Landscapes

Kidnapped, Robert Louis Stevenson

Tarzan of the Apes, Edgar Rice Burroughs

Ender's Game, Orson Scott Card

Riders of the Purple Sage, Zane Grey

Northwest Passage, Kenneth Roberts

The War of the Worlds, H. G. Wells

Private Peaceful, Michael Morpurgo

Slam, Nick Hornby

Lush Life, Richard Price

The Genius, Jesse Kellerman

10 Children's Books I Can't Imagine Not Having Read

Little Women, Louisa May Alcott

Peter Pan, James Barrie

The Wizard of Oz, L. Frank Baum

Madeline, Ludwig Bemelmans

The Secret Garden, Frances Hodgson Burnett

Alice in Wonderland, Lewis Carroll

The Chronicles of Narnia, C. S. Lewis

A Wrinkle in Time, Madeline L'Engle

Anne of Green Gables, Lucy Maud Montgomery

The Five Little Peppers and How They Grew, Margaret Sidney

10 Windows into the Middle East

Someone to Run With, David Grossman

The Reluctant Fundamentalist, Mohsin Hamid

In Other Rooms, Other Wonders, Daniyal Mueenuddin

The Bus Driver Who Wanted to Be God, Etgar Keret

A Woman in Jerusalem, A. B. Yehoshua

Monsieur Ibrahim and the Flowers of the Koran, Eric-Emmanuel Schmitt

Naphtalene: A Novel of Bagdad, Alia Mamdouh

Persepolis, Marjane Satrapi

Habibi, Naomi Shihab Nye

The Space Between Our Footsteps: Poems and Paintings from the Middle East, Naomi Shihab Nye

10 Books to Challenge (and Delight) Your Very Best Readers

Cloud Atlas, David Mitchell

Snow, Orhan Pamuk

Europe Central, William T. Vollman

The Notebook, Agota Cristof

A Short History of Tractors in Ukranian, Marina Lewycka

The Secret Agent, Joseph Conrad

Truth and Beauty, Ann Patchett

Out Stealing Horses, Per Petterson

1599: A Year in the Life of William Shakespeare, James Shapiro

Reality Hunger, David Shields

10 Most Commonly Stolen Books from My Classroom Library

Cut, Patricia McCormick

The Rose That Grew from Concrete, Tupac Shakur

Always Running, La Vida Loca, Luis Rodriguez

Push, Sapphire

Chew on This, Eric Schlosser and Charles Wilson

American Gods, Neil Gaiman

Motherless Brooklyn, Jonathan Lethem

The Amazing Adventures of Kavalier and Clay, Michael Chabon

Maximum Ride, James Patterson

Special Topics in Calamity Physics, Marisha Pessl

10 Books That I Wish Had Been Written When I Was a Young Reader

The Magician's Elephant, Kate DiCamillo

Harry Potter and the Half-blood Prince, J. K. Rowling

The Hunger Games, Suzanne Collins

The First Part Last, Angela Johnson

Curious Incident of the Dog in the Night Time, Mark Haddon

Animal's People, Indra Sinha

Fingersmith, Sarah Waters

The Elegance of the Hedgehog, Muriel Barbery

The White Tiger, Aravind Adiga

The Thousand Autumns of Jacob de Zoet, David Mitchell

Whether I shall turn out to be the hero of my own life, or whether

that station will be held by anybody else, these pages must show.

WITH RIGOR FOR ALL
STUDY GUIDE

Good Night, Good night! Parting is such sweet sorrow,

that I shall say good night till it be morrow.

Life appears to me too short to be spent in nursing

animosity or registering wrongs.

Prejudices, it is well known, are most difficult to eradicate

from the heart whose soil has never been loosened or fertilized

by education: they grow there, firm as weeds among stones.

Questions for Discussion

1. Carol Jago argues that if students find the books in your curriculum difficult to read, the solution is not to seek simpler texts but to help students become better readers. What do you think? What are the biggest obstacles you face? How can teachers work together to overcome these obstacles?

2. What concerns you the most about implementing the Common Core Standards for reading literature in your classroom? What resources do you need to help your students meet these standards? Think of ways to articulate these needs to the powers that be.

3. In Chapter 5, Carol Jago talks about making literature study "blissfully productive," capitalizing on the way video games appeal to students. How does the way in which lessons typically are structured work against blissful productivity? Can you think of ways to bring more pleasure into the study of literature?

4. Chapter 6 explores Mihaly Csikszentmihalyi's research on working in a state of flow: "Contrary to what we usually believe, the best moments in our lives are not the passive, receptive, relaxing times—although such experiences can also be enjoyable, if we have worked hard to attain them. The best moments usually occur when a person's body or mind is stretched to its limits in a voluntary effort to accomplish something difficult and worthwhile." (1990, 3) Can you think of a time when you experienced this state of flow? Think of a time you observed students so absorbed in their reading and writing that the task itself seemed to disappear. What was it about the lesson that produced this effect?

5. One often hears the mantra that "assessment drives instruction." How can you apply the ideas from Chapter 7 on testing that teaches to use classroom assessment to drive instruction in a productive rather than abusive direction?

6. Social networks and the online environment are a natural part of our students' lives. How can we integrate technology into the teaching of literature in ways that enhance rather than distract from deep reading and deep thinking?

7. Think about your own experiences as a reader in middle and high school. What were the formative moments in your own literacy development, moments that possibly led to your becoming an English teacher? How might these experiences inform your instruction?

A Conversation with Carol Jago

Q You write with such passion about teaching literature, Carol. What's the source of this passion?

I take inspiration from Sin'ichi Suzuki. Most of us know the Suzuki Method as a way to teach very young children to play the violin or piano, but Suzuki was actually an educational philosopher. He wrote, "I want to make good citizens. If a child hears fine music from the day of his birth and learns to play it himself, he develops sensitivity, discipline and endurance. He gets a beautiful heart." (Suzuki 1986) That's what I want for my students, too.

Q But how does this apply to teaching literature?

The Suzuki method employs immersion, encouragement, small steps, imitating examples, internalizing principles, contributing novel ideas to help students develop mastery over their instrument. The kind of instruction I've described in With Rigor *employs these same ideas to the teaching of literature. When each step is small, students develop confidence. Though the goal—for example, reading* Macbeth—*may be hugely challenging, students feel they are making progress along the way.*

Q What do you think gets in the way of students making progress?

One issue is students' feelings of helplessness in the face of a big, fat book. Another is that students haven't heard fine literature from the day of their birth. Suzuki was onto something very important when he recognized the critical importance of immersion in music—or poetry, or stories—in the development of future musicians and readers.

I also think that it is really hard to sell books you don't love to students. If I were in charge of the world, I'd give teachers a great deal more professional discretion in which books they teach. Right now, our choices are often limited by whatever books we can find in the school bookroom. What if public access to online texts made the universe of literature available at no charge to every teacher and student? Call me a dreamer, but if the Vatican can put its library online, why can't the Library of Congress?

Q But isn't that a dangerous idea, giving every teacher total control over his or her curriculum?

I don't envision decisions about which texts to teach being made in a vacuum. English departments should put their heads together, read together in book clubs that include parents and students, talk

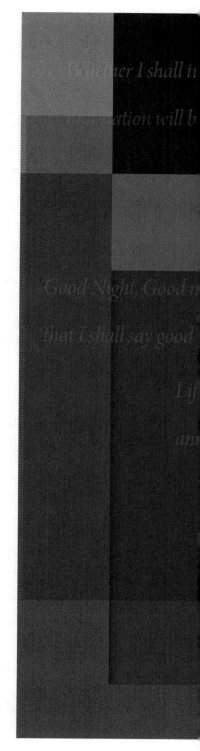

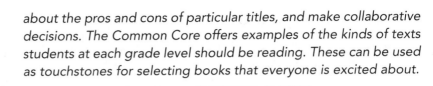

about the pros and cons of particular titles, and make collaborative decisions. The Common Core offers examples of the kinds of texts students at each grade level should be reading. These can be used as touchstones for selecting books that everyone is excited about.

Q I've got to ask. When do you find time to read?

There's always time to do the things we love. Where do kids find twenty hours a week to play video games? Where do dog owners find time for walking their beloved pets? I'm never without a book—and haven't been since I was about nine years old. It's a habit—one I try to instill in my students. Lately I see everyone on a bus or train staring into a phone rather than into a book. Do people really have so many friends with so many important things to say? Or is it for distraction? I'd rather be distracted by art, by literature.

Your Turn: Guidelines for Curriculum Development

These guidelines for applying the concepts presented in *With Rigor for All* to your curriculum will be most valuable if used collaboratively in professional learning communities or within an English department study group.

1. Select a piece of literature you would like to include in your curriculum. Reread the Common Core's explanation of the three-part model for measuring text complexity in Appendix A.

Three-Part Model for Measuring Text Complexity

(1) *Qualitative dimensions of text complexity.*

(2) *Quantitative dimensions of text complexity.*

(3) *Reader and task considerations.*

www.corestandards.org/the-standards

2. Consider the book you have chosen in light of the Common Core explanations regarding text complexity and the text exemplars for the grade level where you plan to teach the book. Develop a rationale for why you believe this piece of literature is a good choice for students.

3. Identify the textual challenges that this piece of literature is likely to pose for students. Using the index of *With Rigor for All* to help you find what you are looking for, find instructional suggestions for helping students overcome these obstacles. Common challenges include: vocabulary, syntax, background knowledge, figurative language, story structures, and length.

4. Adapt the ideas presented in *With Rigor for All* to the piece of literature for which you are developing curriculum. Remember to consider students with special needs who might need differentiated instruction.

5. Create a flexible pacing guide for lessons and homework reading assignments. Design both formative and summative assessments for the unit.

6. Acquire a class set of copies of the new book and have one teacher in your study group pilot teaching the text using the lessons the group has drafted.

7. Develop an instrument the teacher and students involved in the pilot program can use to offer feedback on the book and lessons. Survey questions you might use or adapt include:

   • What do you think you will remember one year from now from your reading of this book? Why?

   • Identify portions of aspects of the book that you had difficulty comprehending. What did you do when you found that you didn't understand what you had read?

   • Which of the assignments did you find most valuable, most fun? What did they help you learn?

   • Were there any assignments you felt were busywork or pointless? Please explain.

   • How did you feel about the way your learning was assessed? Was it too easy, too hard, or just right?

   • Would you recommend this book for next year's class? Why or why not?

8. After the pilot program is complete, examine and discuss feedback from the teacher and students who participated. Look for specific suggestions from the survey to help you determine what revisions need to be made to the sample lesson plans.

9. Read and discuss student performances on the summative assessment. Do they demonstrate the kind of learning you had hoped to see? Do they demonstrate progress toward the Common Core Standards in reading literature?

10. Revise, revise, revise! Email Carol Jago at cjago@caroljago.com if you have questions or concerns.

11. Implement (or jettison) the proposed addition to your literature curriculum.

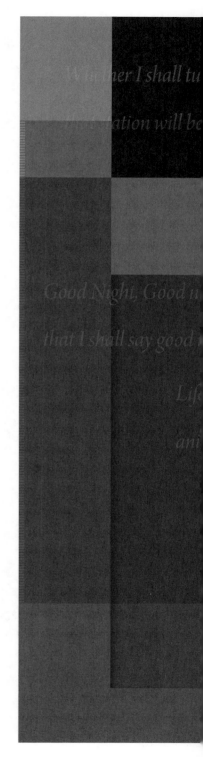

WORKS CITED

ACT. 2006. "Reading Between the Lines: What the ACT Reveals About College Readiness in Reading. April. www.act.org/research/policymakers/pdf/reading_report.pdf.

Adams, Marilyn. 2010–2011. "Advancing Our Students' Language and Literacy: The Challenge of Complex Texts." *American Educator* 34, no. 4 (Winter): 3–10.

Allensworth, Elaine. 2005. "Graduation and Dropout Trends in Chicago: A Look at Cohorts of Students from 1991 to 2004." Consortium on Chicago School Research. January. http://ccsr.uchicago.edu/content/publications.php?pub_id=61.

Alliance for Excellent Education. 2006. "Double the Work: Challenges and Solutions to Acquiring Academic Language and Literacy for Adolescents." www.all4ed.org/publication_material/reports/double_work.

———. 2010. "The Crisis in America's High Schools." www.all4ed.org/about_the_crisis/impact.

Anonymous. 2001. *Beowulf: A New Verse Translation.* Trans. Seamus Heaney. New York: W. W. Norton and Company.

———. 2008. *Beowulf.* Trans. Burton Raffel. New York: Signet Classic.

Arnold, Matthew. 1932. *Culture and Anarchy.* Cambridge: Cambridge University Press.

———. 1994. "Buried Life." *Dover Beach and Other Poems.* New York: Dover Publishers.

Associated Press. 2010. "MO School Board Keeps Ban on Sherman Alexie Book." September 11. www.nativetimes.com/index.php?option=com_content&view=article&id=4239:mo-school-board-keeps-ban-on-sherman-alexie-book&catid=50&Itemid=26.

Baker, Nicholson. 2010. "Painkiller Deathstreak: Adventures in Video Games." *The New Yorker* August 9: 52–59.

Beck, Isabel, M. McKeown, and L. Kucan. 2002. *Bringing Words to Life: Robust Vocabulary Instruction*. New York: The Guildford Press.

Berthoff, Ann E. 1999. "Reclaiming the Active Mind." *College English* 62, no. 1 (July): 671–80.

Birkerts, Sven. 1994. *The Gutenberg Elegies, The Fate of Reading in an Electronic Age*. New York: Fawcett Columbine.

Booth, Wayne. 1998. "The Ethics of Teaching Literature." *College English* 61, no. 1 (September): 41–55.

Brodsky, Joseph. 1987. Nobel Prize acceptance speech. http://nobelprize.org/nobel_prizes/literature/laureates/1987/brodsky-speech.html.

Brooks, David. 2010. "Faustus Makes a Deal." *The New York Times* June 21. http://www.nytimes.com/2010/06/22/opinion/22brooks.html?_r=1.

Campbell, Joseph. 1973. *The Hero with a Thousand Faces*. Princeton: Princeton University Press.

Carr, Nicholas. 2008. "Is Google Making Us Stupid?" *The Atlantic*. July/August.

———. 2010. *The Shallows: What the Internet Is Doing to Our Brains*. New York: W. W. Norton & Company.

Chase, William M. 2009. "The Decline of the English Department." *The American Scholar* August.

Common Core State Standards for English Language Arts & Literacy in History/Social Studies, Science, and Technological Subjects. 2010. National Governors Association and the Council of Chief State School Officers. www.corestandards.org/the-standards.

Compton, Robert, executive producer. 2007. *Two Million Minutes*. www.2mminutes.com/about.asp.

Csikszentmihalyi, MIhaly. 1990. *Flow, The Psychology of Optimal Experience*. New York: Harper Row.

Cunningham, Michael. 1998. *The Hours*. New York: Farrar, Straus and Giroux.

Cyr, Ellen M., ed. 1901. *Cyr's Fourth Reader*. New York: Ginn & Co. Publishers.

Davies, Robertson. 1990 (1960). *A Voice from the Attic: Essays on the Art of Reading*. New York: Penguin.

———. 1992. *The Tanner Lectures on Human Values:* Volume 13. Edited by Grethe B. Peterson. University of Utah Press.

Delpit, Lisa. 1995. *Other People's Children*. New York: The New Press.

Dickens, Charles. 1994. *Great Expectations*. Oxford: Oxford University Press.

Dillard, Annie. 1988. *An American Childhood*. New York: Harper Perennial.

Dostoevsky, Fyodor. 1996. *Crime and Punishment*. Trans. Constance Garnett. New York: Modern Library.

Eco, Umberto. 1994. *Six Walks in a Fictional Woods*. Cambridge, MA: Harvard University Press.

Ellison, Ralph. 1980. *Invisible Man*. New York: Vintage Books.

Epstein, Joseph. 1997. *The Norton Book of Personal Essays.* New York: W. W. Norton & Company.

Finn, Checker. 2010. "A Sputnik Moment for U.S. Education." *Wall Street Journal* December 8. Opinion. http://online.wsj.com/article/SB10001424052748 704156304576003871654183998.html.

Gaiman, Neil. 2008. *The Graveyard Book.* New York: Harper Collins Publishers.

Gardner, John. 1989. *Grendel.* New York: Vintage Books

Gregory, Marshall. 2009. *Shaped by Stories: The Ethical Power of Narratives.* South Bend: University of Notre Dame Press.

Hart, Betty, and Todd R. Risley. 2003. "The Early Catastrophe: 30 Million Word Gap by Age 3." *American Educator* Spring.

Hayakawa, S. I. 1991. *Language in Thought and Action.* 5th edition. New York: Harvest Original.

Homer. 1997. *The Odyssey.* Trans. Albert Cook. New York: W. W. Norton & Company.

Johnson, Annie Fellows. 1921. *Little Colonel's House Party.* Boston: C. H. Simonds Company.

Jones, Sam. 2010. "Tom Stoppard in Warning Over Decline of 'Printed Page' in Education." *The Guardian* Monday, 21 June. www.guardian.co.uk/stage/2010/jun/21/tom-stoppard-warning-printed-page?INTCMP=SRCH.

Kaiser Family Foundation study. 2010. "Generation M2: Media in the Lives of 8- to 18-Year-Olds." January. www.kff.org/entmedia/mh012010pkg.cfm.

Kipling, Rudyard. 1987. *The Jungle Book.* New York: Penguin Classics.

Kohn, Alfie. 1995. "An Interview with Alfie Kohn." *California English* 1, no. 2 (Winter): 26–27.

Longfellow, Henry Wadsworth. 2000. *Henry Wadworth Longfellow: Poems and Other Writings.* New York: Library of America.

Mackey, Margaret. 1997. "Good-Enough Reading: Momentum and Accuracy in the Reading of Complex Fiction." *Research in the Teaching of English* 31, no. 4 (December): 428–58.

McKeown, M. G., I. L. Beck, R. C. Omanson, and M. T. Pople. 1985. "Some Effects of the Nature and Frequency of Vocabulary Instruction on the Knowledge of Use of Words." *Reading Research Quarterly* 20: 522–35.

Mitchell, Margaret. 1993. *Gone with the Wind.* New York: Warner Books.

Nagy, W. E., R. C. Anderson, and P. A. Herman. 1987. "Learning Word Meanings from Context During Normal Reading." *American Educational Research Journal* 23: 237–70.

Newkirk, Thomas. 2010. "The Case for Slow Reading." *Educational Leadership* 67, no. 6 (March): 6–11.

Niles, John D. 1998. "Reconceiving Beowulf: Poetry as Social Praxis." *College English* 61, no. 2 (November): 143–66.

Nussbaum, M. 2010. *Not for Profit: Why Democracy Needs the Humanities.* Princeton: Princeton University Press.

Pressley, Michael, and Peter Afflerbach. 1995. *Verbal Protocols of Reading: The Nature of Constructively Responsive Reading.* Hillsdale, NJ: Erlbaum.

Prose, Francine. 1999. "I Know Why the Caged Bird Cannot Read." *Harper's Magazine* September.

Quindlen, Anna. 1998. *How Reading Changed My Life.* New York: The Library of Contemporary Thought, The Ballentine Publishing Group.

Rabinowitz, Peter J., and Michael W. Smith. 1998. *Authorizing Readers: Resistance and Respect in the Teaching of Literature.* New York: Teachers College Press.

Rawlings, Marjorie Kinnan. 1985. *The Yearling.* New York: Charles Scribner's Sons.

Reid, Louann. 1997. "Rationales for Challenged Materials." *Statement 33,* no. 3 (Summer): 2.

Rosenberg, Howard. 1999. "The Invisible Man Is Alive and Well." *Los Angeles Times/ Calendar* July 25.

Rosenblatt, Louise. 1983. *Literature as Exploration.* New York: The Modern Language Association.

Scholes, Robert. 1989. *Protocols of Reading.* New Haven: Yale University Press.

Shakur, Tupac. *2Pacalypse Now.* Jive, 1998, compact disc.

Solzhenitsyn, Alexander. 2005. *One Day in the Life of Ivan Denisovich.* New York: Farrar, Straus and Giroux.

Stahl, Stephen. 2003. "How Words Are Learned Incrementally over Multiple Exposures." *American Educator* Spring: 18–19.

Steinbeck, John. 1992. *The Grapes of Wrath.* New York: Penguin Classics.

Stevenson, Robert Louis. 1998. *Treasure Island.* New York: Signet Classics.

Stillman, Peter K. 1985. *Introduction to Myth.* 2d edition. Portsmouth, NH: Boynton/Cook Publishers, Inc.

Stone, Irving. 1987. *The Agony and the Ecstasy.* New York: Signet.

Stotsky, Sandra. 1999. *Losing Our Language.* New York: The Free Press.

———. 2010. "Literary Study in Grades 9, 10, and 11: A National Survey." *Association of Literary Scholars, Critics, and Writers* no. 4 (Spring).

Strickland, James. 1997. "What Would You Recommend?" *California English* 3, no. 1 (Fall): 16–17.

Suzuki, Shinichi. 1986. *Nurtured by Love*, 2ed. Translated by Waltraud Suzuki. Plano, TX: Suzuki Method International.

Tatum, Alfred. 2009. *Reading for Their Lives: (Re)Building the Textual Lineages of African American Adolescent Males.* Portsmouth, NH: Heinemann.

Thoreau, Henry David. 1975. "Sunday." *A Week on the Concord and Merrimak Rivers.* Edited by Carl F. Hovde, William Howarth, and Elizabeth Hall Witherell. Princeton: Princeton University Press.

Vygotsky, L. S. 1962. *Thought and Language*. Edited and translated by E. Hanfmann and G. Vakar. Cambridge, MA: MIT Press.

Wilson, August. 1986. *Fences*. New York: New American Library.

Wilhelm, Jeff. 1997. *"You Gotta BE the Book."* New York: Teachers College Press.

Willingham, Daniel. 2006–2007. "Ask the Cognitive Scientist: The Usefulness of *Brief* Instruction in Reading Comprehension Strategies." *American Educator* (Winter): 39–46.

———. 2010. *Why Students Don't Like School: A Cognitive Scientist Answers Questions About How the Mind Works and What It Means for the Classroom.* San Francisco: Jossey-Bass.

Wolf, Maryanne. 2007. *Proust and the Squid: The Story and Science of the Reading Brain.* New York: Harper.

Zehr, Mary Ann. 2010. "Well-Known ELL Researcher Says Simplified Texts Are a Problem." *Education Week*. September 30. http://blogs.edweek.org/edweek/learning-the-language/2010/09/lily-wong_fillmore_simplified.html.

Zimmerman, Susan, and Chryse Hutchins. 2003. *Seven Keys to Comprehension: How to Help Your Kids Read It and Get It.* New York: Three Rivers Press.

INDEX